Ex Libris

Jane Mecom

BOOKS BY CARL VAN DOREN

ANTHOLOGY

The Portable Carl Van Doren

HISTORY

The Great Rehearsal
Mutiny in January
Secret History of the American Revolution
American Scriptures

AUTOBIOGRAPHY

Three Worlds

BIOGRAPHY

Benjamin Franklin · *Swift* · *Thomas Love Peacock*
James Branch Cabell · *Sinclair Lewis*

FICTION

Other Provinces · *The Ninth Wave*

LITERARY HISTORY AND CRITICISM

The American Novel · *Contemporary American Novelists*
The Roving Critic · *Many Minds*
American and British Literature Since 1890
(with Mark Van Doren)
What Is American Literature?

BOOKS EDITED BY CARL VAN DOREN

The Cambridge History of American Literature
Modern American Prose · *An Anthology of World Prose*
Benjamin Franklin's Autobiographical Writings
Letters and Papers of Benjamin Franklin and Richard Jackson
The Letters of Benjamin Franklin and Jane Mecom
The Portable Swift

THE PAUL REVERE MALL

Looking from the site of Jane Mecom's house in Unity Street toward
St. Stephen's Church in Hanover Street.

BENJAMIN FRANKLIN
1706 – 1790
PRINTER, SCIENTIST, PHILANTHROPIST,
DIPLOMAT AND STATESMAN
A MAN OF TOWERING EMINENCE

AS PUBLISHER OF POOR RICHARD'S ALMANAC
HE PROVIDED AMERICA IN ITS UPBUILDING
WITH A PRACTICAL PHILOSOPHY
AND ENRICHED ITS COMMON SPEECH
WITH A WEALTH OF PROVERBS

HE BELIEVED THAT REASON AND WORK
ARE THE PATHS TO PROGRESS

HIS HUMOROUS, REALISTIC, FAR-RANGING MIND
THE LIBERALISM OF HIS POLITICAL AND SOCIAL PHILOSOPHY,
THE MANIFOLD SERVICES HE RENDERED TO HIS FELLOWMEN,
MADE HIM ONE OF THE GREATEST AMERICANS

HE LIVED AS A BOY AT THE CORNER OF UNION
AND HANOVER STREETS.
THE HOUSE FORMERLY STANDING IN UNITY STREET
AT THE HEAD OF THIS MALL WAS OWNED BY HIM
AND OCCUPIED BY HIS SISTERS

* * *

BRONZE PLAQUE
on the south wall of the Paul Revere Mall, commemorating Benjamin
Franklin and mentioning his two sisters Elizabeth Douse and Jane
Mecom, but neither of them by name.

JANE MECOM

❖❖❖❖❖❖❖❖❖

The Favorite Sister of Benjamin Franklin:
Her Life here first fully narrated from
their entire surviving Correspondence

❖❖❖❖❖❖❖❖❖

BY CARL VAN DOREN

1950

THE VIKING PRESS
NEW YORK

SET IN CALEDONIA, BULMER, AND BANK SCRIPT TYPES
AND PRINTED IN U.S.A. BY THE VAIL-BALLOU PRESS, INC.

Preface

THIS book is a belated act of justice to a good, valiant, talented, much-enduring, and charming woman who died more than a century and a half ago. In all those years she has had a shadowy existence in the biographies of Benjamin Franklin, identified as his sister Jane, whose married name was Mecom, who lived in Boston, outlived all their brothers and sisters and Franklin himself, received many letters from him, and wrote many to him. The publication at last of their entire surviving correspondence has brought into history one of the finest known records of friendship between a brother and sister. Jane Mecom could have found in the Book she knew best their best epitaph: they were "lovely and pleasant in their lives, and in their death they were not divided."

The story of Benjamin Franklin and Jane Mecom fills out and enlarges him, and it creates her as a figure that lives with breathing reality. Her story cannot be told without his, for much of what she wrote to him in lost letters now exists only in his replies. But she is the heroine, and this biography of her tells her story as separately as possible, with the light always falling upon her in her early and middle years of tragedy and hardship and in her final years of a triumph and peace she had never dared to expect.

To find out her story it has been necessary to dig round the roots of life in Boston in the eighteenth century: the life of small tradesmen, small boarding houses, small domestic ways and means of livelihood. Jane Mecom would not have suspected that she left as many traces as she did. But there they are, in old wills and posthumous inventories and newspaper advertisements, not to mention official statistics of births, marriages, deaths, church memberships, appointments to minor offices. Ransacked, with Jane Mecom in mind, they and her correspondence give up a moving story of her marriage to an obscure, poor, and ailing saddler, and her harassed widowhood; of her twelve children of whom two went mad and all but one died before her; of her boarding house and, from time to time, her millinery shop; of the help from her brother in Philadelphia which alone kept her circumstances from being desperate; of her flight from occupied and besieged Boston and her eight years as refugee; of her eventual return to live secure in her old age and to write such letters in those years as no other woman of her lifelong handicaps is known ever to have written.

The story makes Jane Mecom more visible and audible than any other woman of that American century who did not herself live close to large events in the career of a husband. But Jane Mecom is more than a contribution to history. She is an addition to the number of persons who persist in the world's memory, like characters of fiction or heroes of legend. Her time and countless obscure women of her time live in her. She is a document, for no fiction is here admitted to her story. She is flesh and blood, a woman timeless and perennial, fitted after so long by the story of her life and the simple magic of her words to enter any company in the wide world of which, living, she saw so little.

CONTENTS

JANE MECOM'S
BOSTON

Illustrations, Facsimiles, and Map

Photograph by Edward Fitzgerald

SITE OF JANE MECOM'S HOUSE

in Unity Street at the head of the Paul Revere Mall extending from
Unity to Hanover Street. The small walled garden encloses the ground
formerly occupied by the Douse-Franklin-Mecom house, No. 19 Unity
Street, at the right of the spectator, and also the site of No. 21, at the
spectator's left. Part of Christ Church is shown at the rear of the garden.

THE BLUE BALL

The house at the corner of Union and Hanover Streets which long stood upon the site of Josiah Franklin's wooden house and continued to use the original Blue Ball as a sign. The sign is still preserved by The Bostonian Society. The photograph was made about 1855, before the house was destroyed.

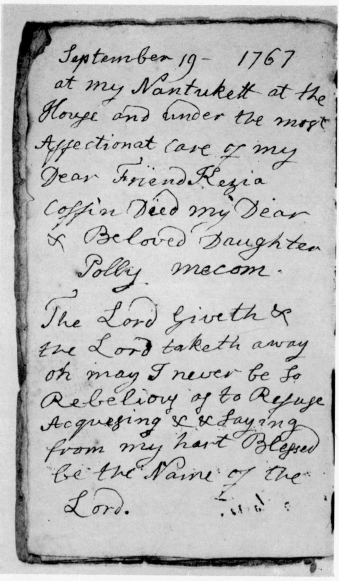

THE DEATH OF POLLY MECOM
Last page of Jane Mecom's manuscript "Book of Ages."

Stiring with a Small switch made on Purpose to m
it & keep it Smoth on the top take care to let you
frame Stand on a Level et care be taken when
is in that it & Is not Soyd nonany thing Fall in
it to Brake the Surface, in the morning it
will be cool anou to cut eys, if it Should Stand
too long it will be diffuilt & also if you cut in
too warm it will not be Smoth yet to wayp &
crack, when you are going to cut it take out t
take un Key your frame & take it of, Peal down
the Lining quite to the boton Plank and mar
it all Round the thicknes Each of a cake with a
marks made on Purpose with Spears in it
when you have Leveled the top mark it a long
across the Size of the cakes, & if you have a
Stamps Stamps it, then Proceed to cut of the
Slab with a Small wier fixed to a round Stick at
Each End to Pull by, then hold it up on Edg
put it throw Length ways Laying won half a
a time in a gage made on Purpos just to this
nes or the cake with the Stamps Downwards
and Smoth it to a Level then lay it on a
table to be cut in to Several cakes & Proceed
to do the other in like maner.

If for Sale as Each Cake ought to be of Equal
weight we have a Small gage to put Each in & Pu
it fill

FOR MAKING CROWN SOAP

The last page of Jane Mecom's manuscript recipe, with drawings
possibly by Benjamin Franklin. The words "hand Gauge" are almost
certainly in his hand.

View of the BRIDGE *over* CHARLES RIVER.

Opened with elaborate ceremonies on June 17, 1786, and described by Jane Mecom in a letter to Franklin of July 21. "It is really a charming place. They have leveled the rising ground that led to it and nicely paved it, that at some distance as you approach to it it is a beautiful sight, with a little village at the other end, the new buildings all new. The prospect on each side is delightful. I frequent go on the Hill for sake of the prospect and the walk. . . . I have once walked over it." The illustration is from the *Massachusetts Magazine* (Boston) for September 1789.

View) of the Town of BOSTON from Breeds Hill in CHARLESTOWN.

Jane Mecom lived during the last ten years of her life just behind Christ Church, marked by the middle of the three spires seen in the picture at the spectator's left. The illustration is from the *Massachusetts Magazine* for June 1791.

S.E. Prospect from an Eminence near the Common, Boston.

View of Boston looking south from the Common and showing at the spectator's right the Neck as Jane Mecom saw it in her travels. The illustration is from the *Massachusetts Magazine* for November 1790.

View of the Colleges at Cambridge. Massachusetts.

Harvard College as seen by Jane Mecom in her later years. She lived with her daughter in Cambridge for several months in 1782–1783. The illustration is from the *Massachusetts Magazine* for June 1790.

(ABOVE) Jane Mecom's autograph on the half-title of her copy of Franklin's *Experiments and Observations on Electricity made at Philadelphia in America* (London, 1769), which he sent her with his letter of February 23 in that year.

(BELOW) Augustin Dupré's medal struck in 1784 in honor of Franklin, who sent a Dupré medal either of this year or of 1786 to Jane Mecom with a letter of September 4, 1786.

B.FRANKLIN, L.L.D. F.R.S.

Born at Boston in New England, Jan 17 1706.

NON SORDIDUS AUCTOR NATURÆ VERIQUE.

"YOUR PROFILE DONE MORE TO YOUR LIKENESS"

Jane Mecom called this in a letter to her brother in May 1786, "than any I have heretofore seen." It appeared as the frontispiece to Franklin's *Political, Miscellaneous, and Philosophical Pieces*, published in London in 1779.

Boston Jan. 19 - 1790

This Day my Dear Brother compleats his
84th year you can not as Old Jacob Say few and
Evel have they been, Exept those wherein you have Endured
Such grevious Torments Laterly, yours have been filld
with Enumereble Good works, Benifits to your felow
creaturs, & Thankfulnes to God; that notwithstanding
the Distressing circumstance before mentioned, yours
must be Esteemed a Glorious Life, Great Increece
of Glory & Happines I hope Await you, may God
mitigate your Pain & continue your Patience yet many
years for who that Know & Love you can Bore the
thoughts of Serviving you in this Gloomy world. —

I Esteem it very Fortunat that cousin John
williams is Returning to Philadelphia again & will
take a Keg of Souns & Tounges by Land as there is
no vesel Likely to go till march I have Tested them
& think them very Good Shall as long as they are Keept
-able Send you fresh & fresh as I have opertunity.

I am as you Supose Six years younger than you
Are being Born on the 27th march 1712 but to
Appearance in Every ways Light as much older,
we have Hitherto a very moderat Winter but
I do not Attempt to go abroad my Breath but
Just Serves me to go about the House without
Greate Pain & as I am comfortable at Home I Strive
to be content.   Remember my Love to
      your children from yr Affectionate
Sister

      Jane mecom

JOHN LATHROP, D.D.

Jane Mecom's pastor during the last ten years of her life, helpful to
her in many ways, and one of the executors of her will. From Chandler
Robbins, *A History of the Second Church, or Old North, in Boston. To
which is added a History of the New Brick Church* (Boston, 1852).

BIRTHDAY LETTER

from Jane Mecom to Benjamin Franklin, January 17, 1790. Printed
with modern spelling and punctuation in Chapter 10 of this biography.

JANE MECOM'S BOSTON

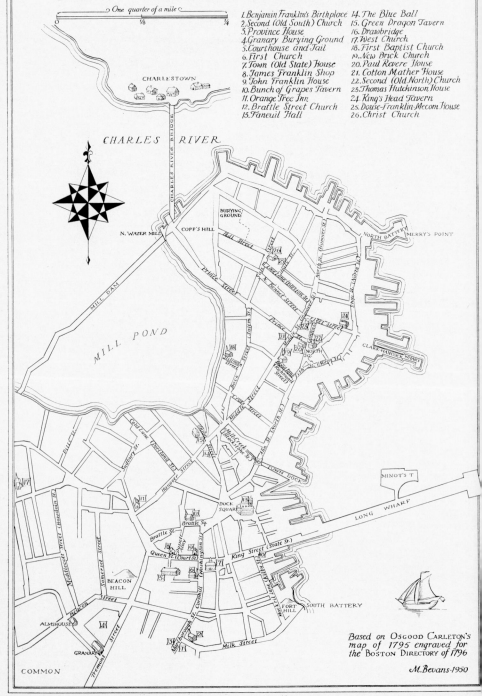

One quarter of a mile

1. Benjamin Franklin's Birthplace
2. Second (Old South) Church
3. Province House
4. Granary Burying Ground
5. Courthouse and Jail
6. First Church
7. Town (Old State) House
8. James Franklin Shop
9. John Franklin House
10. Bunch of Grapes Tavern
11. Orange Tree Inn
12. Brattle Street Church
13. Faneuil Hall
14. The Blue Ball
15. Green Dragon Tavern
16. Drawbridge
17. West Church
18. First Baptist Church
19. New Brick Church
20. Paul Revere House
21. Cotton Mather House
22. Second (Old North) Church
23. Thomas Hutchinson House
24. King's Head Tavern
25. Douse-Franklin-Mecom House
26. Christ Church

CHARLESTOWN

CHARLES RIVER

MILL POND

COMMON

Based on Osgood Carleton's map of 1795 engraved for the Boston Directory of 1796

M. Bevans-1950

JANE MECOM

A Lowly Dwelling

J ANE MECOM, youngest sister of Benjamin Franklin, was
seventy-five when she wrote her only surviving words
about their childhood in their father's house, with its sign of
the Blue Ball, at the southeast corner of Union and Hanover
Streets, Boston. "It was indeed a lowly dwelling we were
brought up in, but we were fed plentifully, made comfortable
with fire and clothing, had seldom any contention among us,
but all was harmony—especially between the heads; and they
were universally respected, the most of the family in good
reputation. This is still happier living than multitudes enjoy."

Benjamin, the tenth of Josiah Franklin's sons, was six years
old when Jane, the seventh daughter, was born on March 27,
1712. She was eleven when her restless brother ran away from
Boston to begin in Philadelphia his immense career. After that
the two were together only seven times in their long lives,
sometimes briefly, never more than a few months at a time.
But neither increasing years nor separating miles nor the
world of difference in their circumstances could ever touch
their early affection except to deepen and widen it.

Though Josiah Franklin was the father of seventeen children, seven by his first wife and ten by his second, the household in which Jane grew up was not large for Boston in that
age. Three brothers had died years before in infancy, and a

fourth at sixteen months had been drowned in a tub of suds. Three other brothers and four sisters were married before she was born or while she was still a small child. One of her brothers had left his trade for the sea; another was learning the printer's trade in London. After she was four there were only two children regularly in the house besides Benjamin and Jane: the colorless Lydia who was between them in age, and the amiable if plain Sarah who was seven years older than Benjamin.

Their Uncle Benjamin Franklin, when Jane was eleven, spoke of her as a "good humored child" in a letter to a niece named Jane in England. Not another characterizing word has come down about the first fourteen years of the Jane Franklin of Boston, the liveliest and brightest of the Franklin daughters, the favorite of her gifted brother Benjamin, and apparently of all the family. Benjamin, telling about the holiday on which he bought his whistle, says that when he came home, "whistling all over the house . . . disturbing all the family," his "brothers, sisters, and cousins" found out what he had paid for it and teased him because it was four times too much; but Jane was only a year old. When he blew soap bubbles, as he says he did, Jane may have tried to catch them in her excited hands. But, as little girls were then brought up in Boston, she would not have been permitted to run with her brother and his friends along Union Street, past the Green Dragon Tavern, to the Mill Pond where Benjamin learned to swim and manage boats; or go with him farther than to some nearby pasture to fly the kites he made.

Years later Franklin in a letter to his sister quoted two lines—

> A man of words and not of deeds
> Is like a garden full of weeds—

from "an ancient poet whose works we have all studied and copied at school long ago." This seems to imply that Jane went to school, but there is no other reference to it. If she was sent at all, it was to some private school for small children, where she learned a little reading, writing, and arithmetic, and perhaps needlework and embroidering. Benjamin went to the school of George Brownell in Hanover Street when Jane was three or four. Jane may have gone to the same school later. She spelled badly all her life, but she seems always to have read as much as she could find time for, and she wrote amazing letters.

Her brother, telling about the Franklin household in his *Autobiography*, spoke chiefly of the father. "He had an excellent constitution of body, was of middle stature, but well set, and very strong; he was ingenious, could draw prettily, was skilled a little in music, and had a clear pleasing voice, so that when he played psalm tunes on his violin, and sung withal, as he sometimes did in an evening after the business of the day was over, it was extremely agreeable to hear. He had a mechanical genius too, and, on occasion, was very handy in the use of other tradesmen's tools; but his great excellence lay in a sound understanding and solid judgment in prudential matters, both in private and public affairs. In the latter, indeed, he was never employed, the numerous family he had to educate and the straitness of his circumstances keeping him close to his trade; but I remember well his being frequently visited by leading people, who consulted him for his opinion in affairs of the town or of the church he belonged to, and showed a good deal of respect for his judgment and advice. He was also much consulted by private persons about their affairs when any difficulty occurred, and frequently chosen an arbitrator between contending parties. At his table he liked to have, as often as he could, some sensible friend or neighbor to converse with, and always took care to start some ingenious or useful topic for discourse, which might tend to improve the minds of his children. By this means he turned our attention to what was good, just, and prudent in the conduct of life; and little or no notice was ever taken of what related to the victuals on the table, whether it was well or ill dressed, in or out of season, of good or bad flavor, preferable or inferior to this or that other thing of the kind."

The youngest son may not have known that before his birth Josiah Franklin had been one of the clerks of the market for a year, charged with preventing misconduct and abuses in the public markets; and for another year a constable, who did police work by day and superintended the town watch at night. The youngest daughter may have forgotten that when she was two her father served a year as one of the tithingmen, special police to keep order inside the churches; and that when she was eight he served another year as one of the scavengers, who were to protect the streets from the rubbish which careless householders were inclined to throw out. These were not elective offices, but burdensome duties imposed by the selectmen in turn upon the citizens. Josiah Franklin no doubt performed his share of the duties, but his world was his house and his shop, where he boiled soap and dipped or molded candles, with the help of his son John and later of Benjamin.

The house at Union and Hanover Streets, which Josiah Franklin had bought just before Jane was born, was then or later four wooden "tenements," the principal one at the corner and the others facing Hanover Street. At first they were separate buildings, joined afterward in some way, perhaps by a common front. The Franklins lived on the corner, with the

Blue Ball on a bracket projecting over the sidewalk. The family had, it is supposed, two rooms on each of two floors, with a cellar and a garret. The center and heart of the house was the kitchen, which was also dining room and living room, for most of the evenings the only room with fire or light—though a candle-maker may have allowed his family more than the three candles a day which were then what plain households limited themselves to.

In the kitchen, breakfast was early and supper late according to the sun in its seasons, but the fare winter and summer was commonly bread and milk or milk with corn-meal mush. Dinner would be some kind of meat, in the form generally of stew from the kitchen pot, or soup, perhaps vegetables or pickles, and a pudding: all these served in two or three large pewter dishes or platters, eaten from pewter plates or wooden trenchers with few knives and no forks. If there were not spoons enough to go round, spoons were passed innocently from mouth to mouth. If there were not chairs enough for all to sit in, the children stood at meals.

The front room on the ground floor was reserved for special occasions, such as when guests came or when fellow members of Josiah Franklin's church met at his house for prayer meetings. The two bedrooms on the second floor were crowded with beds, somewhat like cabins on a ship. There were beds for sleepers who had to go to the unplastered garret, no matter how hot the summer or how cold the winter nights. The toilet, or necessary house, was outside. The shop in which the family made its soap and candles was in one of the buildings on the lot. The whole was probably enclosed with a fence to keep out roaming pigs or other animals, of which the Franklins appear to have owned none themselves. Water was supplied by their own well and pump. The Blue Ball, well known in

Boston, was always spoken of as fronting on Union Street, though its Hanover Street side was almost three times as long.

Years later Franklin remembered thirteen of the sons and daughters "(some of us then very young) all at one table, when an entertainment was made at our house on the occasion of the return of our brother Josiah, who had been absent in the East Indies and unheard of for nine years." Jane cannot then have been more than three or four. And this very entertainment may be one to which their Uncle Benjamin refers in his note on a poem he wrote and read "at first meeting with my nephew Josiah." The homemade quatrains spoke of the dangers of the deep and the goodness of God who preserved the lives of seafaring men, and concluded:

> Adore this God who did us save
> From the much fearèd watery grave,
> And softly set thee on thy land.
> O bless His kind and powerful hand.

But, Uncle Benjamin noted, the sailor nephew was "unaffected with God's great goodness" and the poem was "coldly entertained" by him. That very year, or the next, Josiah perished on some voyage, nobody now knows just how or where.

Uncle Benjamin could speak feelingly about the sea, for he had himself but recently crossed the Atlantic. He was eight years older than his brother Josiah. They had both learned the dyer's trade in England, both were dissenters, and they had kept up a brotherly correspondence between Old England and the New. Uncle Benjamin had suffered misfortunes in London, where his wife and all his ten children had died except the eldest son Samuel, a cutler, who preceded his father to Boston. The father came in 1715 or soon after and lived with his brother for about four years till his son was married and set up housekeeping.

"Our father, who was a very wise man," the nephew Benjamin wrote to Jane long afterward, "used to say nothing was more common than for those who loved one another at a distance, to find many causes of dislike when they came together; and therefore he did not approve of visits to relations in distant places, which could not well be short enough for them to part good friends. I saw a proof of it, in the disgusts between him and his brother Benjamin; and though I was a child I still remember how affectionate their correspondence was while they were separated, and the disputes and misunderstandings they had when they came to live some time together in the same house."

The brothers had not seen each other for more than thirty years when they were reunited. Both past sixty, they were fixed in their characters and opinions. The Blue Ball was hardly large enough for one brother who had to work hard at his trade and another brother who seems to have done nothing but write occasional verses and make notes in his journal and read and speculate. A whole room had to be set aside for him alone. Uncle Benjamin, much taken with his precocious namesake, gave advice about his education and encouraged him to write verse. Josiah told the boy that "verse-makers were usually beggars" and helped him with his prose. But the conflict was never noisy or violent. Jane, less shrewd than her brother, may not even have noticed it. All her life she remembered her Uncle Benjamin with respect and affection.

From the talk of the two old men the children could learn many things about their family in England. There was their father's story about his great-grandfather. "As it was the custom in those days among young men too many times to go to seek their fortune," that far-off Franklin had stopped on his travels first with a tailor, to see if his trade would suit. "But he kept such a stingy house, that he left him and travelled farther, and came to a smith's house; and coming on a fasting day, being in popish times, he did not like it there the first day; the next morning the servant was called up at five in the morning, but after a little time came a good toast and good beer, and he found good housekeeping there. He served and learned the trade of a smith." Ever since then the eldest son in each Franklin family had been bred to the same trade. Josiah Franklin's father, a blacksmith, had lived at Ecton in Northamptonshire. He had been "imprisoned a year and a day on suspicion of his being the author of some poetry that touched the character of some great man." Uncle Benjamin's son was a smith turned cutler, with his sign of the Razor and Crown in North Square. Josiah Franklin's eldest son, also Samuel, had a smithy at the foot of Cross Street which the young Benjamin and Jane had seen. Josiah Franklin's mother had been named Jane, like his youngest daughter. He told the children about his own crossing the Atlantic, so many years ago, with his first wife, Ann Child, and the son and two daughters born in England; and his finding so little need of another dyer in Boston that he became a tallow chandler.

Uncle Benjamin, who had antiquarian tastes, had tried to find out what the name Franklin meant. Some said it meant the Franklins were of French extraction, therefore Franks. Others thought they had belonged to a "line free from that vassalage which was common to subjects in days of old." A man skilled in heraldry had told Uncle Benjamin that there were "two coats of armor, one belonging to the Franklins of the north, and one to the Franklins of the west." Josiah Franklin thought that in view of the Franklin fortunes it was hardly "worth while to concern ourselves much about these things, any farther than to tickle the fancy a little."

Josiah Franklin's wife Abiah could tell the children of the meeting and marriage of her father, Peter Folger of Nantucket, and his wife Mary Morrils. The two, when he was eighteen, had come to America on the same ship; but he was a free youth with his parents, and she was bound to service for a term of years to Hugh Peters, in payment for her passage and support. The Folger family tradition still is, and Abiah Franklin may have heard the facts, that Mary and Peter fell in love on the voyage. But it was nine years before he could get money enough to go to Salem and buy her indenture and claim her in marriage. That was only after Hugh Peters, having returned to England, sent for his wife and children to follow him. Peter now had or had borrowed twenty pounds and made, he said, his best bargain. Of the nine children born to Peter and Mary Folger, the ninth was Abiah, who had come to Boston but still had numerous relations on the island.

On Sundays the Franklins walked, in all but the worst weather, to service at the Third Church, better known as the Old South, which Josiah had attended ever since he came to Boston and to which he had remained faithful after he moved to the North End. They went along Union Street, through Dock Square, along Cornhill (now Washington Street) past the Town House to the meeting house at the corner of Milk Street. Across Milk Street from the Old South was the still lowlier and smaller dwelling in which Josiah Franklin had lived when his household was larger than now, and in which all his American children had been born except possibly Jane. Inside the church the Franklins had their pew at the "return of the gallery," from which the clear voice of the father was pleasing to Judge Samuel Sewall, who led the hymns. One

Sunday when Jane was six Sewall set the familiar York tune
so loosely that the congregation went out of it into St. David's.
Sewall, who had been precentor at the Old South for almost
a quarter of a century, felt that he should give up his post to
"Mr. White, or Franklin might do it very well." But Josiah
Franklin did not become precentor; nor was he elected deacon
that year when he got ten votes but two other candidates got
thirty-seven and nineteen respectively.

When Jane found it difficult to sit through the long ser-
mons of the minister, Joseph Sewall, or his learned associate,
Thomas Prince, it was not because she found theology tire-
some in itself, as her brother Benjamin did. That insatiable
boy, reading all his father's books of divinity, soon came to
think it a waste of time. He pertly proposed to his father that
instead of saying grace before meat at each meal it might be
better to say it once for all over the whole cask in which the
winter's supply was salted and laid down. During the long
morning and evening prayers which Josiah Franklin offered
up, Benjamin studied geography from the four maps which
hung conveniently on the walls of the room. If Jane's eyes
were open, and she saw this, she was troubled, as she was for
years by her beloved brother's unorthodox opinions. She was
a pious child, as well as gentle and charming.

II

The overshadowing later reputation of Benjamin Franklin
has thrown the early lives of his brothers and sisters into a
shade that Jane of course never saw them in. She had nieces
older than she, and by the time she was eleven had become
aunt to half a dozen other nieces and nephews close enough
to her in age to be her playmates. Her brother Josiah set out

on the voyage from which he did not return. Her brother
James returned from London to become a printer in Boston,
at first of ballads and pamphlets and odd jobs on paper; or
on linen, calico, or silk "in good figures, very lively and durable
colors, and without the offensive smell which commonly attends the linens printed here"—as James Franklin announced
in his advertisements. Her brother Samuel, the year James
arrived in Boston, petitioned the selectmen for a license to
retail strong drink, as so many unsuccessful tradesmen did,
and was refused, as so many were. Her eldest sister Elizabeth
went with her first husband, Captain Joseph Berry, to live
in a new "mansion house," so called because it was brick,
though it had only four rooms, in the raw lane later known as
Unity Street. Captain Berry just before Jane's sixth birthday
brought from Maryland the mistaken news that Louis XV
of France had died. Berry himself died on a voyage to Maryland, and his widow was promptly married to another shipmaster, Richard Douse. Jane's brother John, tallow chandler
like his father, when Jane was four or five left Boston with his
wife and son to set up a business in Newport. A regular stage-
coach plied, when the roads were passable, between Newport
and the Orange Tree Inn, at the corner of Hanover and Sud-
bury Streets, in Boston. When Jane was ten her sister Sarah
became the second wife of James Davenport, baker and
tavernkeeper, to become in seven years the mother of five
of his twenty-two children, and to die after nine years of
marriage.

Those "leading people" who visited Josiah Franklin and
asked his counsel have left no names, but the diary of Judge
Sewall speaks of a prayer meeting which he attended at the
Franklin house in April 1713, when Jane was a year old. In
June that year a firm of slave traders advertised "three able

Negro men and three Negro women . . . to be seen at the house of Mr. Josiah Franklin at the Blue Ball in Union Street." In August there were still, or again, three men and two women "to be sold and seen" at the same house. Josiah Franklin owned no slaves himself, but he had some tenement or shed in which he could temporarily take charge of these captives from Africa, at whose dark bewildered faces the baby Jane must have stared or smiled.

From time to time there was an apprentice or a bond servant at the Blue Ball, working all day at the shop or going on errands, eating his meals with the family, sleeping at night on a straw bed in the garret. William Tinsley, bound to Josiah Franklin for a term of years, ran away from his master in July 1722. He was Irish, said the notice in the *New-England Courant* which offered a reward of forty shillings for his apprehension and return to the Blue Ball: "about twenty years of age, of a middle stature, black hair lately cut off, somewhat fresh-colored countenance, a large lower lip, of a mean aspect, large legs, and heavy in his going. He had on, when he went away, a felt hat, a white knit cap striped with red and blue, white shirt and neckcloth, a brown-colored jacket almost new, a frieze coat of a dark color, gray yarn stockings, leather breeches trimmed with black, and round-toed shoes." The notice was printed for three weeks, then nothing more of William Tinsley, the only person whose looks and dress are anywhere described in the records of Jane Franklin's childhood. Not a single likeness has been found of Jane or her parents or any of her brothers and sisters—except of her brother Benjamin, whose face in later years was to be as well known, in countless likenesses, as any face in the world.

It was the youngest son who first brought to the Franklin family a little, unexpected reputation. This was when Jane was six, soon after Benjamin was apprenticed to his brother James the printer. The apprentice, not yet thirteen, began his career with a ballad called "The Lighthouse Tragedy," on a tragic accident which had set all Boston talking. The facts, inaccurate in later histories, were given in the *Boston News-Letter* for the week of November 3–10, 1718. On Monday the third, the account ran, "an awful and lamentable Providence fell out here. Mr. George Worthylake," keeper of the first Boston light, on Great Brewster Island at the entrance to the harbor, "Anne his wife, Ruth their daughter, George Cutler a servant, Shadwell their Negro slave, and Mr. John Edge a passenger, being on the Lord's Day here at sermon, and going home in a sloop, dropped anchor near the landing place, and all got into a little boat or canoe, designing to go on shore; but by accident it overwhelmed, so that they were drowned, and all found and interred except George Cutler." The recovered bodies were brought to Boston, where Cotton Mather of the Second Church (Old North) on November 10 "entertained the flock," he wrote in his diary, with "as useful and pungent a discourse" as he was capable of. Benjamin Franklin may have heard the sermon. In any case, he wrote his ballad, which was printed and "sold wonderfully, the event being recent, having made a great noise." The poet, who had helped print his poem, hawked it through the Boston streets, singing it as he went. Jane had reason to be proud of her favorite brother.

In February 1719 the *News-Letter* had various accounts from roundabout and contradictory sources of the capture and death of the famous pirate Edward Teach, better known as Blackbeard, off the North Carolina coast. Lieutenant Robert Maynard of H.M.S. *Pearl* had gone in command of two sloops with fifty (or fifty-four) men and small arms but no "great guns" against Blackbeard, who had nine (or ten) "great guns" and twenty-one men in a single sloop. Early in the action the officer on Maynard's smaller sloop was killed, the sloop fell astern, and Maynard with about thirty of his men fought alone till almost the end. In one report Maynard boarded Blackbeard, in another Blackbeard was the boarder. In the most spectacular of the accounts, which came from North Carolina to Boston by way of Rhode Island, each man boarded the other in turn.

When the sloops were in hearing, and Teach knew he must fight for his life, he "called for a glass of wine and swore damnation to himself if he either took or gave quarter. Then Lieutenant Maynard told his men that now they knew what they had to trust to, and could not escape the pirate's hands if they had a mind, but must either fight and kill, or be killed. Teach begun and fired several great guns at Maynard's sloop which did little damage; but Maynard rowing nearer Teach's sloop of ten guns, Teach fired some small guns, loaded with swan shot, spike nails, and pieces of old iron in upon Maynard, which killed six of his men and wounded ten; upon which Lieutenant Maynard ordered all the rest of his men to go down in the hold. Himself, Abraham Demelt [De Milt?] of New York, and a third at the helm stayed above deck. Teach, seeing so few on the deck, said to his men, the rogues were all killed except two or three, and he would go on board and kill them himself; so, drawing nearer, went on board, took hold of the foresheet, and made fast the sloops. Maynard and Teach themselves begun the fight with their swords. Maynard making a thrust, the point of his sword went against Teach's cartridge box and bended it to the hilt. Teach broke the guard of it, and wounded Maynard's fingers but did not disable him; whereupon he jumped back, threw away his sword, and fired his pistol, which wounded Teach. Demelt struck in between them with his sword and cut Teach's face pretty much.

"In the interim both companies"—Teach's men, who had come on board after him, and Maynard's, who had scrambled up from the hold—"engaged in Maynard's sloop. One of Maynard's men, being a Highlander, engaged Teach with his broadsword, who gave Teach a cut on the neck. Teach saying 'Well done, lad,' the Highlander replied, 'If it be not well done, I'll do it better.' With that he gave him a second stroke, which cut off his head, laying it flat on his shoulder. . . . Teach's body was thrown overboard, and his head put on top of the bowsprit." Or as another account put it, Maynard carried Teach's head to Virginia, "in order to get the reward offered by the said Colony."

With whatever variation in detail, here was the stuff of as gory a ballad as any the fate of Blackbeard called forth in England or New England. No known ballad on the theme gives the Rhode Island detail of the Highlander and his broadsword, which Benjamin would hardly have left out. His ballad on the vicious Teach seems to have gone the way of his ballad on the virtuous Worthylakes into oblivion. Benjamin, however encouraged by Uncle Benjamin and admired by Jane, gave up ballad-making, as his father advised him to. Nor can it have been difficult for this boy to turn from melodrama in verse to the prose and humor with which he was to raise his family to eminence and give them some share in a history which without him would have been lost.

After Benjamin went at twelve to board with his brother James and to work in his shop, at the corner of Queen (now Court) Street and Dassett Alley (now Franklin Avenue), he was no longer so close to his parents at the Blue Ball, or to

Jane. His tireless reading and thinking made him disagree
with his elders, particularly about religion. It was hard for
his family to understand why so promising a boy should be
so difficult. He fell into the habit of what his father called
"lampooning and libelling" in the company of James Franklin
and his friends, who were joined in what the Mathers called
the Hell-Fire Club as contributors to James' *New-England
Courant,* founded when Jane was nine. With their satirical
pens they vexed the authorities and ridiculed the clergy of
Massachusetts. James, for hinting that the Council was lax in
dealing with pirates along the coast, was sent to prison for a
month. He apologized and was released, but did not sufficiently mend his manners. When, after six months, he was for-
bidden to publish this or any newspaper, and Benjamin in
February 1723 ostensibly became the publisher, the *Courant*
was more guarded but still satirical.

That same month there was a high tide in Boston that affected the family of the Blue Ball, probably brought Benjamin
to its rescue, and owes apparently to him the best record of
the affair. The record was printed in the *Courant* for the week
ending March 4; and it is here reprinted exactly as it was
printed then:

"On Lord's Day, the 24th past, we were surprized with the
extraordinary Heighth of the Tide, which fill'd most of the
Streets as well as Cellars near the Water, insomuch that many
People living in Drawbridge-Street, Union Street, and some
other Places, were carry'd to their Houses in Canoes, after the
Morning Service was over. In some Houses the Water rose so
high in their lower Rooms as that they were oblig'd to run
away with their Meat half dress'd upon their Spits and in their
Potts into some of their Neighbours, or into their upper Rooms,
their Fire being all put out, and the Wood floating about the

Rooms. The Cordwood, Shingles, Staves, &c. were all wash'd off the Wharffs and carry'd into the Harbour, or left in the Streets after the Tide was down. The Water rose so high in the Ship Carpenters Yards, that they fear'd the Vessels would be carried off the Stocks, and made them fast with Ropes to the Tops of the Houses. The Loss sustain'd by this Tide (in Town and Country) is reckon'd by some to be as great as that by the Fire in 1711. Charlestown likewise suffer'd very much; and we hear a great number of Whaleboats have been carry'd from the shore towards Cape Codd, where the Tide was never known to come before. They write from Newport on Rhode-Island, that the Tide has entirely wash'd away several Wharffs, and done great Damage in several Warehouses and Dwelling Houses near the Water."

So far with reporting. But the *Courant* went further, to chaff a rival paper and poke fun at foolish explanations of the calamity.

"By an Article in the Boston News-Letter of Thursday last, we are told, that, *The many great Wharffs which since the last overflowing Tides have been run out into the Harbour, and fill'd so great a Part of the Bason, have methinks contributed something not inconsiderable to the Rise of the Water upon us.* And upon the Authority of this News Letter, some begin to blame the Dutch for damming out the Sea, and sending the Tide over the Atlantick to us: Some more reasonably conclude, that a large Fleet of Ships have been sunk in the Storm upon our Coast, (the Wind blowing hard at North East,) which occasion'd the rising of the Tide. Others have upon this Account, framed a new Hypothesis to resolve the Phænomena of Noah's Flood, and very rationally suppose, that the Antediluvians brought the Deluge upon themselves by running too many Great Wharffs out into their Harbours. So that the Notions (which were not without their *Probabilities*) of Burnet, Warren, Whiston, &c. who were troubled with the Distemper called *Hypothesimania,* seem now less probable than ever."

Benjamin was then seventeen, a stout hand with a canoe, and quick to turn from news to ridicule. At the same time, he was increasingly restive under the control of his brother. The best apprentice in the world had outgrown his status. James, mistaking genius for mere fractiousness, too often beat Benjamin, who later said he had often been "too saucy and provoking." Benjamin appealed to his father, who did what he could to reconcile his two most enterprising sons. The whole household at the Blue Ball was uneasy over the quarrel. The trouble went on all the spring and summer of the year when Jane was eleven. In September Benjamin ran away on board a New York sloop.

That month two sloops cleared from Boston to New York: William Beekman's before the fourteenth, and Arnout Schermerhoorn's before the twenty-first. The *Courant,* announcing the departures on the fourteenth and the twenty-first, was unaware that one of the vessels carried the fugitive. Then on the thirtieth James Franklin informed the public in the *Courant* that he wanted "a likely lad for an apprentice."

The world has long known the story of that flight into triumph. Nobody has thought much of what it cost the family left behind. One morning Benjamin was not in his bed. James had to inquire of his parents. They inquired through the town. Josiah Franklin may have found out that his son had been permitted to go privately on board because Captain Beekman or Captain Schermerhoorn supposed his passenger had "got a naughty girl with child" and dared not leave openly. If the captain believed this, might not the parents suspect it could be true? Benjamin by running away from his apprenticeship had broken a contract with his master which was almost as binding as an enlistment in the Army or Navy. He might be caught and brought back for a reward, like a bond servant or a slave or a criminal. If he had been a contentious doubter in religion in Boston, he might take to worse and worse companions. Quarrelsome at home, he might be lawless abroad. New York was a long way off, with ships on which Benjamin might go to sea and be lost like his brother Josiah. How would the boy make his living? Who would feed and shelter him in strange places? His parents grieved over a son who suddenly seemed to them no more than a child. Jane cried over the loss of the most sympathetic confidant she had ever known, or ever would know.

They naturally did not realize that no boy in America could be more fully trusted than Benjamin to look out for himself in whatever world he might find waiting for him. In this case, his prudence made him cruel to them. For fear of being recalled to Boston, he did not let his family know he had gone to Philadelphia. It was only by chance that his sister Mary's husband, Captain Robert Homes, on a voyage to Delaware learned where Benjamin was. Then in April or May the runaway, ahead of Homes with his news, was home again, with a "genteel new suit from head to foot," near five pounds of silver jingling in his pockets, and the first watch he had ever owned. What was more, he had a letter to his father from Governor Sir William Keith of Pennsylvania, full of smooth flattering things about the young printer, and an offer to be his patron in Philadelphia if Josiah Franklin would advance the money to set his son up in a printing house there.

The prodigal had come home a kind of hero. James was still resentful, and Josiah Franklin declined to invest so much money in a printer so young as Benjamin. But the Boston Franklins in general forgave the runaway and rejoiced in his quick prosperity. He went to call on Cotton Mather, who lived in Hanover Street. Mather, apparently forgiving the boy for his bold pen in the *Courant,* now welcomed him and gave him good advice. When Benjamin returned to Philadelphia he left behind him no such anxiety about his future as on his first leaving.

They did not see him again for nine years. There are no known letters from him to his family written during the almost two years he was in London, where he had gone with false hopes of Governor Keith's patronage. Then on Benjamin's twenty-first birthday, after he had got back to Philadelphia and gone to work as clerk in a store, he wrote what was probably his earliest letter to Jane: the earliest surviving letter to any member of his family. Captain Isaac Freeman, a friend of the Franklins in Boston, had met their youngest son on a voyage to Philadelphia and had given him news of them, particularly of the youngest daughter.

"Dear Sister," Jane read in the letter Freeman brought her, "I am highly pleased with the account Captain Freeman gives me of you. I always judged by your behavior when a child that you would make a good, agreeable woman, and you know you were ever my peculiar favorite. I have been thinking what would be a suitable present for me to make, and for you to receive, as I hear you are grown a celebrated beauty. I had almost determined on a tea table, but when I considered that the character of a good housewife was far preferable to that of being only a pretty gentlewoman, I concluded to send you a spinning wheel, which I hope you will accept as a small token of my sincere love and affection.

"Sister, farewell, and remember that modesty, as it makes

the most homely virgin amiable and charming, so the want
of it infallibly renders the most perfect beauty disagreeable
and odious. But when that brightest of female virtues shines
among other perfections of body and mind in the same person,
it makes the woman more lovely than an angel. Excuse this
freedom, and use the same with me. I am, dear Jenny, your
loving brother, B. Franklin."

Through all the changes and mischances of her life, Jane
cherished this letter. The odd mixture in it of tenderness and
prudence did not seem strange to her: she was a pretty girl
and a tradesman's daughter. Her adored brother had written
to her not as a petted child but as a beloved equal.

2

Ingenious, Sensible, Notable, and Worthy

NONE of Jane Franklin's older sisters had married early, as marriages then went in Boston, and Lydia was still at home at the Blue Ball. But on July 27, 1727, Jane was married at fifteen to Edward Mecom. As if her parents had discountenanced the match, because of her youth or for some other reason, she was married not by one of the ministers of the Old South but by William Cooper of the Brattle Street Church, which her Uncle Benjamin had attended for ten years before his death the past March.

Edward, son of Duncan and Mary Hoar Mecom, came from a family obscurer than the Franklins, and he himself made no mark and left no name except as Jane's husband. Two years after his marriage he was chosen a clerk of the markets; the year after that he became a communicant at Brattle Street, which meant that he and his wife had served their probation and been admitted to full membership. Though he could write, nothing written by him has been found besides a single inexpert signature on a legal document. He begot twelve children, and during his later years was an invalid. All his children but one were named after Jane's parents or brothers or sisters or herself, though her husband also had a sister

Mary and a brother Ebenezer. Edward Mecom's earnings were soon not enough to support his swarming family. By the time the seventh child was born, or possibly before, Jane had begun to take boarders, many of whom were poor themselves.

Whether or not the young couple lived elsewhere at first, they soon came to live at the Blue Ball, either in the corner house with the elder Franklins and Lydia—till she was married to Captain Robert Scott—or in one of the other tenements. Jane, depending in part on her parents for support, repaid them with a devoted and increasing care.

Josiah Franklin kept up a correspondence with his son in Philadelphia. There was little reason for Jane to write to Benjamin or to expect letters from him. In the summer of 1730 her sister Sarah Davenport, not Jane, sent him the news that Jane's first child, Josiah, had died in May not yet a year old. "I had not for two years before," Benjamin said in his reply, "received a line from any relation, my father and mother only excepted. . . . I am sorry to hear of Sister Mecom's loss, and should be mighty glad of a line from her." Benjamin would be glad also of a line from his sister Mary Homes, "who need be under no apprehension of not writing politely enough to such an unpolite reader as I am. I think if politeness is necessary to make letters between brothers and sisters agreeable, there must be very little love among 'em. . . . Please to let me know how Sister Douse is, and give my kind love to her, as also to Brother Peter, and Sister Lydia etc. Dear Sister, I love you tenderly."

All Franklin's sisters were half-afraid of their youngest brother, who seemed to them to be rising so rapidly in the world, and who sent back such "polite" (correct and graceful) letters. But the year after this affectionate reassurance came to Sarah, and was read at the Blue Ball, Jane herself got up courage to write to Philadelphia. She had news enough. Sarah had died; Mary had a cancer of the breast; Jane herself now had a second child, Edward, born in March, though Jane did not write till the end of May. Her letter is lost, but not her brother's prompt answer, in which he adapted his language to her and to her ways of thinking.

The death of their sister, he was sure, would be "regretted by all that knew her, for she was a good woman. Her friends ought, however, to be comforted that they have enjoyed her so long and that she has passed through the world happily, having never had any extraordinary misfortune or notable affliction, and that she is now secure in rest, in the place provided for the virtuous. I had before heard of the death of your first child, and am pleased that the loss is in some measure made up to you by the birth of a second."

He was greatly concerned over the news of Mary Homes' cancer. "I know a cancer in the breast is often thought incurable; yet we have here in town a kind of shell of some wood, cut at a proper time, by some man of great skill (as they say), which has done wonders in that disease, being worn for some time on the breast. I am not apt to be superstitiously fond of believing such things, but the instances are so well attested as sufficiently to convince the most incredulous." If Franklin could borrow the shell he would send it to Jane, "and hope the doctor you have will at least allow the experiment, and shall rejoice to hear it has the accustomed effect. You have mentioned nothing in your letter of our dear parents, but I conclude they are well because you say nothing to the contrary. I want to hear from Sister Douse, and to know of her welfare, as also of my sister Lydia, who I hear is lately married." He had intended to visit Boston that summer, but "printing the paper money" had delayed him and he could only hope to see his family in the fall.

Mary died of her cancer. Franklin could not come to Boston till the summer or fall of 1733 after nine years' absence. When he did, Jane had a third son, named Benjamin after his uncle.

In nine years the Franklin family in Boston had been much reduced in numbers. The sisters Hannah (Eddy) Cole, Anne (married to William Harris), and Mary Homes were dead, as well as Sarah Davenport; and probably their brother Samuel, without a will or any known record. James had gone to Newport, invited by John and several influential citizens there to set up the first printing press in Rhode Island. Their brother Peter had followed, or was to follow, leaving his trade, whatever it was, to be in turn shipmaster and merchant. The only children of Josiah Franklin who were certainly left in Boston were Elizabeth Douse, Lydia Scott, and Jane Mecom.

Jane had two sons, so had Benjamin, married these three years to Deborah Read. He told his sister about William (did Jane know the boy was illegitimate?) and Francis Folger, who still looks sweetly and gravely out of his portrait at a world of which he had time to see so little. Benjamin might meet with the Lodge of Freemasons in Boston and take notes of the Boston methods of preventing fires, but he had come home principally to see his family. At twenty-seven, he was already its second head. If he had little money to give, he had the good sense and loving interest in all their affairs which for Jane were more than money.

Her father had been helping James in Newport. Benjamin on his way back to Philadelphia stopped to visit that brother. "Our former differences were forgotten," Benjamin later wrote, "and our meeting was very cordial and affectionate.

He was fast declining in his health, and requested of me that in case of his death which he apprehended not far distant, I would take home his son, then but ten years of age, and bring him up in the printing business." Franklin agreed, sent the younger James "a few years" to school in Philadelphia, and then took him into the printing house as apprentice. When the elder James died in 1735 Benjamin assisted the widow, who carried on the Newport printing house till her death. This was to make amends for the service Benjamin had run away from before it was completed.

Franklin, who all his life had a genius for drawing like-minded men together in public affairs, had an equal genius for keeping his family in private unity. Though most of the early family letters are lost, the few that survive are full of the warmth which went out from him to all the others and was returned with no resentment of his success, and with grateful adoration from Jane.

For the ten years from 1733 to 1743 the sole records of Jane Mecom, besides one reference to "Sister Jenny" in a letter from Benjamin to their father, are the entries in what she called her "Book of Ages" written in a blank book which still survives. She entered only births and deaths. For this decade there were only births, beginning with her fourth child.

"Ebenezer Mecom Born on May the 2 1735 on friday

Sarah Mecom Born on Tuesday the 28 June 1737

Peter franklin Mecom Born on the Lords day May the 13.1739

John Mecom Born on Tuesday March the 31.1741

Josiah Mecom Born on friday March the 26.1743."

This was the second Josiah born to her, and given the name of her first-born, who had died.

When her brother arrived from Philadelphia in May that

year she could show him six nephews and a niece. Edward, twelve, had begun to learn the saddler's trade from his father. Benjamin, ten, was the quickest at his books. His mother hoped, and her brother thought, that this boy could become a printer. A place might be found for him with Franklin's partner, James Parker, in New York, not so far off as Philadelphia. What Franklin had done for James' son he could do for Jane's.

Jane, for whom letters were still rare and difficult, had many questions to ask about her brother's family in Philadelphia. His William, who was about her Edward's age, liked to read and had a pony. Francis had died of smallpox at four. His small tombstone called the child "The DELIGHT of all that knew him." Deborah assisted in her husband's store and the post office, and was to have another child this coming August. The fine soap, of a clear green color and stamped on each cake with a crown, which John Franklin had made in Newport and was now making in Boston, sold well in Philadelphia. Here was "domestic chitchat like common folks," as Jane later called it, in which she could feel happily at ease with her clever brother who had become the most prosperous of all the Franklins who had ever lived in England or America.

Reserved to others, he told her about his profitable newspaper and his popular almanac; the books he published and the public printing he did; the library and the fire company in which he had a guiding hand; the "Pennsylvanian Fireplace" he had invented but left to later times to call the Franklin stove. He was postmaster at Philadelphia and clerk of the Pennsylvania Assembly. He hoped to establish an American Philosophical Society, to unite "ingenious men" from every colony in the promotion of useful knowledge. During this brief stay in Boston he made his first acquaintance with electricity when he saw Adam Spencer perform electrical experiments on apparatus he had brought from Scotland. So far as the future was concerned, this was the most important thing Franklin did on that visit. To Jane the important thing was her eager conversations with Benjamin.

Josiah Franklin, listening to his son, could quote again what he had often quoted before: "Seest thou a man diligent in his business? he shall stand before kings." But both Josiah and his wife, and particularly Jane, were still troubled by Benjamin's cheerful rationalism and his infrequent attendance at church. The Great Awakening, preached by George Whitefield and Jonathan Edwards, was alive in New England. Jane, who had no philosophy but her simple religion, felt that her brother set too much value on good works and not enough on faith. Perhaps Jane did not, while he was in Boston, have the courage to tell him what she thought about his want of faith. But after his return to Philadelphia she wrote him a letter, now missing, to which he replied in late July.

"Dearest Sister Jenny," he began, "I took your admonition very kindly, and was far from being offended at it. If I say anything about it to you, 'tis only to rectify some wrong opinions you seem to have entertained of me, and that I do only because they give you some uneasiness which I am unwilling to be the occasion of. You express yourself as if you thought I was against worshipping of God, and believed good works would merit heaven: which are both fancies of your own, I think, without foundation. I am so far from thinking that God is not to be worshipped that I have composed and wrote a whole book of devotions for my own use; and I imagine there are few, if any, in the world so weak as to imagine that the little good we can do here can *merit* so vast a reward hereafter. There are some things in your New England doctrine and worship which I do not agree with, but I do not therefore condemn them, or desire to shake your belief or practice of them. We may dislike things that are nevertheless right in themselves. I would only have you make the same allowances and have a better opinion both of morality and of your brother. Read the pages of Mr. Edwards's late book entitled *Some Thoughts concerning the present Revival of Religion in N. E.* from 367 to 375; and when you judge of others, if you can perceive the fruit to be good, don't terrify yourself that the tree may be evil, but be assured it is not so; for you know who has said: 'Men do not gather grapes of thorns or figs of thistles.' I have not time to add but that I shall always be your affectionate brother."

Then, remembering that Jane had felt hurt by something their sister Elizabeth or Lydia had said, Franklin added a postscript. "It was not kind in you to imagine when your sister commended good works she intended it a reproach to you. 'Twas very far from her thoughts."

Already, and throughout her life, Jane was quick to see offense where none was intended. Her brother, who told her she had a "miffy temper" and said it was a Folger not a Franklin trait, took it for granted in her, smiled at it, and smiled again at her when she suddenly was as quickly contrite and apologetic.

In January 1745 Josiah Franklin died, leaving, the *Boston News-Letter* said, to "a numerous posterity the honor of being descended from a person who, through a long life, supported the character of an honest man." His widow in her new mourning, Jane carrying her ninth child unborn, the sisters Elizabeth and Lydia, John, who had come back from Newport to live in Boston, and other relatives and friends followed the

patriarch's body to the Granary Burying Ground, listened
to the services consigning him to the cold earth, and went
home to the Blue Ball, where there were two gallons of wine
for the funeral and the will which he had made the past October.

"I give to my loving wife Abiah Franklin," the will said, "all
the incomes or rents of my whole estate and goods and the
use of the two rooms we now live in, allowing the lodgers
to be in as now it is used, she allowing out of it the interest
that will be due to my creditors while she lives." The widow
continued in her two rooms for the rest of her life, with the
Mecoms apparently in the same house and various "lodgers"
in the other tenements. Years later Captain Hugh Ledlie of
Hartford remembered that he had lodged with Jane Mecom,
on his visits to Boston, as early as 1742 in her "honored mother's lifetime." There were two shops in the tenements, one of
them Edward Mecom's.

Benjamin Franklin, writing to his sister when he heard the
news from Boston, said: "Dear Sister, I love you tenderly for
your care of our father in his sickness." And he went on to
tell her and her husband that they might now send their son
Benjamin to New York to begin his apprenticeship with James
Parker, Printer, on Hunter's Key. Franklin would hear, Jane
would be glad to know, from his partner about the boy every
week. "You will advise him to be very cheerful, and ready to
do everything he is bid, and endeavor to oblige everybody,
for that is the true way to get friends."

Then for seven years few words from Jane Mecom except
the records of her children in her "Book of Ages."

"Jane Mecom Born on Saturday April the 12.1745

James Mecom Born on July 31.1746. Died november the
30 1746

Mary Mecom Born febry the 29 1747–8
Abiah Mecom born augst 1st 1751 died April the 23 1752."

After Josiah Franklin's death his widow wrote to her son in Philadelphia by almost every post, and he replied to her, knowing Jane would read his letters.

He told them of the arrival in Philadelphia in September 1749 of his nephew Josiah, a baker, son of Sarah Davenport, with his wife. "I met them the evening before at Trenton, thirty miles off, and accompanied them to town." The young couple had spent Saturday and Sunday at Franklin's house and gone into their own on Monday. Deborah had been to see them every day and, Franklin wrote, "I suspect has fallen in love with our new cousin"—that is, Sarah Billings of Boston, Josiah's wife. (Jane, like her brother, spoke of the latter part of the afternoon as "evening" and of a niece or nephew as "cousin.") In October of that year came *Poor Richard* for 1750; and with it a gold moidore, a Portuguese coin worth about twenty-seven shillings, which Benjamin asked his mother "please to accept towards chaise hire, so that you may ride warm to meetings this winter." Benjamin had ordered a horse collar from Edward Mecom, and Abiah Franklin thought her son-in-law had been slow in sending it. "I doubt not but Brother Mecom," Benjamin said, "will send the collar as soon as he can conveniently."

In April 1750 the mother and sister in Boston heard from Franklin that his son William was "now nineteen years of age, a tall proper youth, and much of a beau." His daughter Sarah was six, a fine girl, "extremely industrious with her needle, and delights in her work. She is of a most affectionate temper, and perfectly dutiful and obliging to her parents, and to all. Perhaps I flatter myself too much, but I have hopes that she will prove an ingenious, sensible, notable, and worthy

woman, like her Aunt Jenny." Here was compliment enough
to keep Jane warm for days.

On October 14, 1751, Abiah Franklin wrote her only letter
that has survived. "I am glad to hear," she said in it, "that you
are so well respected in your town for them to choose you
alderman, although I don't know what it means nor what
the better you will be of it besides the honor of it. I hope you
will look up to God, thank Him for all His good providences
toward you. He has prospered you much in that place and I
am very thankful for it. I hope you will carry well so that
you will be liked in all your posts. I am very weak and short-
breath so that I can't sit to write much although I sleep well
a-nights and my cough is better and I have a pretty good
stomach to my victuals."

To this Jane added her earliest surviving lines in all the correspondence with her brother. "P. S. Mother says she an't
able and so I must tell you myself that I rejoice with you and
bless God for all your prosperity and doubt not but you will
be greater blessings to the world as He bestows upon you
greater honors."

Later in the month William arrived in Boston with a letter
to Jane from his father recommending the youth to her "moth-
erly care and advice. . . . My compliments to my new niece,
Miss Abiah," Franklin went on, "and pray her to accept the
enclosed piece of gold, to cut her teeth; it may afterwards buy
nuts for them to crack."

That winter smallpox came terribly to Boston on board a
ship from London. Before the disease had run its course nearly
an eighth of the sixteen thousand inhabitants had fled the
town, and about five hundred had died. In April 1752 Abiah
Franklin wrote two lost letters to say that her youngest granddaughter was very ill. "The account you give of poor little

Biah grieves me," her son replied, "but I still hope the best. However, God's will must be done. I rejoice that the rest of Sister's children and Brother Davenport's are likely to escape so well." He sent an order on the postmaster of Boston for six pistoles (Spanish gold coins worth about eighteen shillings). "I beg Sister to accept four of them, and you the other two."

But before this letter could reach the Blue Ball, little Abiah Mecom died; and two weeks later Abiah Franklin followed her namesake to the grave. Jane and Edward Mecom wrote Franklin the news of their mother. "I thank you," Benjamin replied, "for your long continued care of her in her old age and sickness. Our distance made it impracticable for us to attend her, but you have supplied all. She has lived a good life, as well as a long one, and is happy." Because the Boston postmaster had delayed paying the order on him, Franklin now sent six pistoles in cash.

The gold pieces he sent from time to time were only incidents in his regular generosity to his Boston relations. He lent money to his father and supported his sister Elizabeth in her last years. But this and his steady assistance to the Mecoms were little in comparison with the patient time Franklin spared out of his busy life for aid and advice to his Franklin and Mecom and Davenport nephews, not to mention remoter kinsmen who might be in need.

II

The year of little Abiah's death saw the end of Benjamin Mecom's apprenticeship in New York. He had been restless and full of complaints in letters to his mother. When he had the smallpox, at fifteen, the Negro woman who was supposed to be his nurse neglected him, he said. He did not like the clothes that Parker bought for him. He resented being asked to go on petty errands. He tried to run away to sea, and justified himself by making charges against Parker and his wife.

Jane in the summer of 1748 sent her brother some of the boy's letters, with letters from her to him and to Parker, for Franklin to read and forward. Those letters are lost, but his reply quieted some of Jane's alarms, even if it painfully reminded her of the days when her brother Benjamin had been a restless apprentice quarreling with his master, who was her brother James.

Parker's wife, Jane read, had herself been sick when Benny was, and her child also. All Benny charged his nurse with was that she "never brought him what he called for directly, and sometimes not at all. He had the distemper favorably, and yet I suppose was bad enough to be, like other sick people, a little impatient, and perhaps might think a short time long, and sometimes call for things not proper in his condition.

"As to clothes, I am frequently in New York, and I never saw him unprovided with what was good, decent, and sufficient. I was there no longer than March last, and he was then well clothed, and made no complaint to me of any kind. I heard both his master and mistress call upon him on Sunday morning to get ready to go to meeting, and tell him of his frequently delaying and shuffling till it was too late, and he made not the least objection about clothes. I did not think it anything extraordinary, that he should be sometimes willing to evade going to meeting, for I believe it is the case with all boys, or almost all. I have brought up four or five myself"— as apprentices in Philadelphia—"and have frequently observed that if their shoes were bad, they would say nothing of a new pair till Sunday morning, just as the bell rang, when if you asked them why they did not get ready, the answer was prepared: 'I have no shoes,' and so of other things, hats and the like. Or if they knew of anything that wanted mending, it was a secret till Sunday morning, and sometimes I believe they would rather tear a little than be without the excuse.

"As to going on petty errands, no boys love it, but all must do it. As soon as they become fit for better business, they naturally get rid of that, for the master's interest comes in to their relief. . . . In the meantime, I should be glad if Benny would exercise a little patience. There is a Negro woman that does a great many of those errands."

Jane was terrified by the news that Benny had tried to run away from his apprenticeship and enlist on a privateer. She thought his master's harsh treatment to blame. Her brother, she found, did not agree with her. "When boys see prizes brought in," from raids on French shipping in the current war, "and quantities of money shared among the men, and their gay living, it fills their heads with notions that half distract them, and put them quite out of conceit with trades and the dull ways of getting money by working. This I suppose was Ben's case, the *Catherine* being just before arrived with three rich prizes; and that the glory of having taken a privateer of the enemy, for which both officers and men were highly extolled, treated, presented, etc. worked strongly upon his imagination, you will see, by his answer to my letter, is not unlikely. I send it to you enclosed. I wrote him largely on the occasion; and though he might possibly, to excuse that slip to others, complain of his place, you may see he says not a syllable of any such thing to me. My only son, before I permitted him to go to Albany," with a Pennsylvania regiment raised against Canada, "left my house unknown to us all, and got on board a privateer, from whence I fetched him. No one

imagined it was hard usage at home that made him do this.
Every one that knows me thinks I am too indulgent a parent
as well as master.

"I shall tire you, perhaps, with the length of this letter,"
which in fact Jane found completely absorbing, "but I am the
more particular in order, if possible, to satisfy your mind
about your son's situation. His master has, by a letter this
post, desired me to write to him about staying out of nights,
sometimes all night, and refusing to give an account where
he spends his time, or in what company. This I had not heard
of before, though I perceive you have." Benny had complained to his mother that he had been whipped for the offense. Franklin did not wonder at the punishment. "If he was
my own son, I should think his master did not do his duty
by him if he omitted it, for to be sure it is the high road to
destruction. And I think the correction very light, and not
likely to be very effectual, if the strokes left no marks."

Only the year before Hogarth in London had published
his famous history in pictures of the Industrious Apprentice
and the Idle Apprentice, in which Tommy Idle took to bad
company and ran away to sea and ended up on the gallows,
while Frank Goodchild won his master's favor and his daughter and rose to be Lord Mayor. And here in Boston Jane
Mecom thought of Benny as at the dangerous crossroads in
New York.

There was comfort for her in her brother's conclusion to
his long letter. "I have a very good opinion of Benny in the
main, and have great hopes of his becoming a worthy man,
his faults being only such as are commonly incident to boys
of his years; and he has many good qualities, for which I love
him."

For four years Benny Mecom caused his mother less anxiety. Then came what looked like sudden good fortune. Franklin had sent one of his journeymen, Thomas Smith, to Antigua to set up the first printing press and first newspaper in the Leeward Islands. Smith died in the summer of 1752, and Franklin immediately thought of sending Benny to take the vacant place. Though the boy was not yet twenty, he was a skilled workman and eager to be independent, the only printer on an island in the opulent Caribbean.

The matter was hurriedly arranged. Jane Mecom knew only that Benny was to go, and had to wait for details till after he had set out from Philadelphia late in August. Then she and her husband had a letter from Franklin that answered the questions she would most like to ask.

"That island," her brother assured her, "is reckoned one of the healthiest in the West Indies. My late partner there enjoyed perfect health for four years, till he grew careless and got to sitting up late in taverns, which I have cautioned Benny to avoid; and have given him all other necessary advice I could think of, relating to both his health and conduct, and hope for the best. He will find the business settled to his hand, a newspaper established, no other printing house to interfere with him or beat down his prices, which are much higher than we get on the continent. He has the place on the same terms with his predecessor, who I understand cleared five or six hundred pistoles during the four years he lived there."

If Benny could clear as much he would have a larger income, for himself alone, than his parents and eight brothers and sisters had in Boston. His mother, worried most about Benny's health and his conduct, was happy in the thought that her son had such prospects, and full of grateful love for her brother who had made them possible.

"Mr. Parker," the letter went on, "though he looked on Benny as one of his best hands, readily consented to his going on the first mentioning of it. I told him Benny must make him satisfaction for his time"—that is, the unexpired service of the apprenticeship. "He said he would leave that to be settled by me; and Benny as readily agreed with me to pay Mr. Parker as much as would hire a good journeyman in his room. He came handsomely provided with apparel, and I believe Mr. Parker has in every respect done his duty by him, and in this affair has really acted a generous part; therefore I hope if Benny succeeds in the world he will make Mr. Parker a return beyond what he had promised. I suppose you will not think it amiss to write Mr. and Mrs. Parker a line or two of thanks; for notwithstanding some little misunderstandings, they have on the whole been very kind to Benny. . . .

"After all, having taken care to do what *appears to be for the best,* we must submit to God's providence, which orders all things *really for the best.*"

Jane Mecom may not have learned from her brother that in the month after this letter he told the world, in *Poor Richard,* about the lightning rod and sent to the Royal Society in London his account of the electrical kite he had flown in Philadelphia. But in November she received from him the news of "Benny's arrival" in Antigua, for whom Franklin said he had been "some time in pain." The affair was not working out so smoothly as it had promised to, and the young man was already restless and dissatisfied. "That you may know the whole state of his mind and his affairs, and by that means be better able to advise him, I send you all the letters I have received from or concerning him. I fear I have been too forward in cracking the shell and hatching the chick to the air before its time. . . . In my opinion, if Benny can but be prevailed on to behave steadily, he may make his fortune there. And without some share of steadiness and perseverance he can succeed nowhere."

The long dreary tragedy of Benjamin Mecom's life had begun, with its sporadic interludes of hopeful energy, and its longer and longer spells of lassitude and despair.

3

As Our Number Grows Less

WHEN in July 1753 Benjamin Franklin arrived in Boston on his decennial visit he found his sister Jane in awe of him as she had never been before. The apprentice of thirty years before who in the *New-England Courant* had ridiculed the "beetle-skulls" of Harvard now received from Harvard the earliest of his academic honors. "On Monday last," she read in the *Boston Gazette* of July 31, "the Corporation of Harvard College met at Cambridge, and taking into consideration the great genius of Benjamin Franklin, of Philadelphia, Esq., for learning, the high advances he has made in natural philosophy, more especially in the doctrine and experiments of electricity, whereby he has rendered himself justly famous in the learned world, unanimously voted him a degree of Master of Arts, which vote was the day following as fully confirmed by the Overseers of that Society, and on Friday the President presented him a diploma therefor." And here in the crowded shabby Blue Ball was the overwhelming diploma, with Benjamin showing his sister his name in Latin (*Dominus Benjamin Franklin Armiger, de Philadelphia americanâ*) and the praise of his achievements which had carried his merited fame not only to England but also to France (*undè apud doctos non in Britannia solum, verùm etiam in Galliâ, fama percrebuit, et ipse in orbe literato optimè meruit*). All this for Jane was wonder and magic, and she was diffident in the face of such mysteries.

And yet there was no change in Benjamin's concern for her and the welfare of her family. Of her daughters, the pretty Sarah was sixteen, the eight-year-old Jane had little airs and graces, and Mary (called Polly) seemed obedient, responsible, and charming beyond her five years. The sons were all working at their trades or learning them.

Edward, the eldest, was a saddler like his father, whom the son helped in the shop at the Blue Ball. Ebenezer was learning to be a baker under the instruction of his uncle James Davenport, who kept the King's Head Tavern in Fleet Street and near it had a bakeshop with three ovens which was said to be "the best accommodated for business of any in the Province." John Mecom was learning the goldsmith's trade from his cousin William Homes at the sign of the Key in Ann (now North) Street. Peter was living with his uncle John Franklin, working at the family trade of tallow chandler and learning to make crown soap. The Mecoms could not afford the usual fees then charged for teaching three boys their trades. The father had taught his own trade to Edward and was beginning to teach it to Josiah, who was ten. The others must get their education from obliging kinsmen, as Benny had got his from his uncle Benjamin.

Peter's prospects seemed the best, for John Franklin was the most prosperous of all the Boston Franklins. His first wife, Mary Gooch, had died, and his second, Elizabeth Gooch Hubbart, brought him the well-furnished mansion house in Cornhill which had belonged to her former husband, along with three sons and two daughters. John Franklin had an excellent library, family portraits (including one of himself and one of his brother Benjamin), a chaise and harness, a slave named Caesar, and a work house with all the utensils needful in his trade. Now past sixty, he was afflicted with a bladder stone and feared he had not long to live; but there was reason for Jane to think that his will would contain some provision for her son Peter.

Though the Franklin of Philadelphia had come to Boston on the business of the colonial post office, of which he was now controller, he had time for all his family. To his sister Elizabeth Douse, whose husband died that year, he began or continued to advance money, secured by a mortgage on her house. There is no mention in 1753 of the colorless Lydia Scott, but she was alive and had a daughter, and Franklin saw them both. He saw a good deal of his brother John, who was a partner in a company organized to manufacture glass, with glass-workers imported from Germany, at a site on Boston Harbor which is now a part of Quincy. At the urging of John, and also of their brother Peter who may have been in Boston that summer, Benjamin bought lots in "Germantown" and arranged to build two small tenements to be let to workers. And it was with Benjamin's advice that the Blue Ball was finally advertised for sale in the July of this visit to Boston.

The Blue Ball, with its four tenements, was a burden for Jane to manage, and there were the interests of the other heirs to be considered. The house and household goods were appraised at a little over three hundred pounds, and sold for less. But there were debts due from the estate, Jane's share was only one-ninth of the whole, and her husband owed at least a year's rent to the executors. It might be better, even though a whole house elsewhere would rent for more than the Mecoms paid for their part of the Blue Ball, for them to move to an establishment all their own.

This had probably been decided when Franklin set out for Philadelphia, to receive another honorary degree of Master of Arts from Yale, in September, on his way. Before or not long after the Blue Ball was sold to William Homes the following April, the Mecoms moved to an unidentified house in Hanover Street, near the busy Orange Tree Inn. It seemed an advantageous situation. Travelers who found no room at the Inn or the Inn's prices too high might come instead to Mrs. Mecom's boarding house.

A later inventory throws some light on the house and its arrangement. The front room on the ground floor with its three windows was Edward Mecom's shop, where he worked when he was well enough at making or mending saddles or other harness, with the help of his eldest son. Behind the shop was the dining room, with nine chairs round the table, a small fireplace, a desk, a looking glass and pictures on the wall, and the family silver: three large spoons, nine teaspoons, and the tea tongs. The dishes, all pewter, were in the kitchen at the rear, with its larger fireplace and equipment for cooking, nine old brass and iron candlesticks to light the family and the lodgers to bed, and an old warming pan. The two or more bedrooms on the second floor or in the garret were crammed with five old bedsteads, feather beds, straw beds, a servant's bed and bedding, an old couch, seven chairs, two chests, a "case" of drawers, and one looking glass. Some of these things had come from the Blue Ball and were worn from years of use, by the lodgers who came and went and by the growing Mecom children.

Besides the Mecoms there was a servant without a surname in the record, called by Jane in her letters merely "Old Sarah" and apparently as much dependent as servant. Of the lodgers only one for these early years is known by name: the picturesque Captain Ledlie, officer of a Connecticut regiment, occasionally a police officer, a land speculator, and long the promoter of a new road to be built from Hartford to Boston. He came regularly whenever he was in town, drawn by the landlady's friendly welcome and her many "acts of kindness." During the sessions of the Assembly in Boston various country members boarded with Jane Mecom, pleased with her modest rates and not troubled by the plain fare or the crowding, which was what they expected away from home, and what some of them were used to at home. What more could a traveler want than a warm fire in the kitchen, and enough food on the table, and a bed to sleep in at night—alone if he was lucky, with one or two other travelers if that had to be?

It is not certain whether, when Franklin returned to Boston late in 1754, he stopped at the new boarding house. If he did, he was the most eminent guest the house ever had. Since his last visit he had been awarded the Copley gold medal of the Royal Society. He had been appointed, with William Hunter of Virginia, Joint Deputy Post Master and Manager of all His Majesty's Provinces and Dominions on the Continent of North America. The tallow chandler's son was an officer of the Crown, in effect the postmaster-general of the continental colonies. He was now on a tour of inspection of New England, selecting post roads and post riders, arranging for ferries to carry the mails over wide unbridged rivers, making contracts and issuing commissions from Connecticut to New Hampshire.

From Jane Mecom's house, if Franklin stopped there, he went several times to confer with Governor William Shirley at the Province House in Cornhill, near which Josiah Franklin had had a small shop many years ago. Possibly it was in the Hanover Street boarding house that Franklin wrote the famous letters to Shirley which in that December philosophically and prophetically outlined, as no one else had yet done, the grounds of conflict between the colonies and the royal government. When Franklin was not in attendance on the governor he might be meeting with various scientific friends and correspondents in Boston: the young James Bowdoin, merchant and careful observer of luminosity in sea water; John Winthrop, the Harvard astronomer; and Dr. John Perkins, the Mecoms' family physician. Letters between each of them and Franklin had already been published, or were to be, in London in various issues of his *Experiments and Observations.*

Jane Mecom, full of love and diffidence, watched her brother coming and going, equally at ease in affairs of the post office or principles of government or subjects of scientific inquiry or the domestic problems of the Mecoms. This year he revealed a new interest. At John Franklin's house he had two eager young admirers in Elizabeth Hubbart, John's stepdaughter, and Catharine Ray of Block Island, one of whose sisters was married to one of Elizabeth's brothers. Each of the young women fell chastely, filially, in love with him, though he was roughly twice the age of either; and he responded with the half-paternal, half-philandering gallantry in which he now took his masterly first steps. While he and Catharine Ray were forming a lifelong attachment, so were she and Jane Mecom, whom Catharine loved not only because she was Franklin's sister but also because she was so full of love and life. That very year Franklin as Poor Richard said: "If you would be loved, love and be lovable."

The year, and the visit, were marked by an event which drew all the Boston Franklins together and gave the town one of its lasting monuments. A new tombstone appeared in the Granary Burying Ground, of Pennsylvania marble, on which was cut, by an unknown young Philadelphia "Artist," an Epitaph which millions of eyes have read during two centuries. It said, as copied a little later by Benjamin Mecom:

JOSIAH FRANKLIN
And
ABIAH, HIS WIFE
Lie here interred
They lived lovingly together in Wedlock
Fifty-five Years
And Without an Estate or any Gainful
Employment,
By Constant Labor and Honest Industry
(with God's Blessing)
Maintained a large Family
Comfortably,
And brought up thirteen Children and
Seven Grand-Children
Reputably
From this Instance, Reader,
Be encouraged to Diligence in thy Calling
And distrust not PROVIDENCE.
He was a pious and prudent Man,
She a discreet and virtuous Woman
Their youngest Son
In filial Regard to their Memory
Places this Stone
J. F. born 1655 died 1744
A. F. born 1667 died 1752.

Of all the Boston Franklins, Jane Mecom was the one most certain to remember that their father had died in 1745 (that is, 1744/5); and the one most likely to remember that he himself had given the year of his birth as 1658. And Jane could know, what nobody in many years has ever stopped to think about, who were the seven grandchildren whom the elder Franklins had brought up reputably. More than twice that number of grandchildren survived Josiah and Abiah Franklin, of whom nine were Mecoms. But Benjamin Mecom had been educated by his uncle Benjamin and Peter by his uncle John. The seven referred to in the Epitaph were without much doubt the remaining Edward, Ebenezer, Sarah, John, Josiah, Jane, and Mary, all of them brought up at the Blue Ball under the roof and with the assistance of their grandparents. The stone placed over their graves by their youngest son perpetuated also the special gratitude of their youngest daughter.

Benjamin Mecom, with his first printing of the Epitaph four years later, commended the skill with which the letters were formed, then added: "though he that cut the stone is now in the same state with those whom it is intended to commemorate. He was lately shot dead by lurking Indians on the frontiers of Pennsylvania"—in the war which drew Benjamin Franklin into the affair of Braddock's expedition against the Ohio Indians and took Franklin himself on his own small military campaign against the Indians nearer home.

At the end of December Franklin, to be accompanied by Catharine Ray as far as Rhode Island, departed for Philadelphia. On January 2 the *Boston News-Letter* announced that "the post office is now kept at Mr. John Franklin's in Cornhill," which meant that Franklin's brother had been commissioned postmaster at Boston. The same issue of the newspaper reprinted, from the *Gentleman's Magazine* in

London, a favorable notice of Benjamin Franklin's *New Experiments and Observations on Electricity.* The next month Joseph Hiller, a jeweler, announced a course of demonstrations of the newly discovered "electrical fire" to be given at his house near the Blue Ball. Anyone might attend for one pistareen (the old Spanish peseta, worth a little more than a Massachusetts shilling) for each lecture.

In spite of these pleasant reminders of a famous brother, Jane Mecom found the boarding house dull without him and his friends, whom she saw less frequently after he had gone. There was now only the daily round of her small affairs, her children, and her boarders. In July her son Edward was married to Ruth Whittemore, and went to live in a house nearby. Besides his saddler's shop they had, then or soon, a small stock of miscellaneous goods to sell at retail: cowskins, spice, crown soap, mustard seed, raisins, butter, garters, silk handkerchiefs, tobacco and short pipes, needles, and both New England and West Indian rum. A daughter was born to them the year following, but died in infancy. Edward himself was soon ailing, apparently tubercular, and often unable to work.

At the end of January 1756 John Franklin died of his painful malady. In his will he left to his wife the use of "all the utensils" of his business, the copper cauldron, the iron furnace, and other implements, and of his Negro named Caesar; all these to go after her death to Peter Franklin Mecom, then not seventeen, and another apprentice, James Barker, "equally between them." Peter was also to have a suit of clothes, "but not mourning." Then in a codicil there was a further provision: "And whereas I have given to my wife the use of my Negro named Caesar during her natural life, I now give my executors liberty to dispose of him if he behaves ill, and my said wife to have the use of the money, and at her decease to be divided equally between my kinsmen Peter Franklin Mecom, James Barker, and John Mecom." For Jane Mecom there was a pair of "Silver Canns with my arms upon them."

From Benjamin Franklin, just home from his campaign, came words that forecast all the future relations between him and his sister. "As our number grows less, let us love one another proportionably more." But with it came other words that were disturbing. "Benny, I understand, inclines to leave Antigua. He may be in the right. I have no objection."

II

Much disturbed, Jane Mecom wrote asking why her son was leaving Antigua and pouring out her thanks for all her brother had done. The letter went to Philadelphia, followed him to Virginia where he had gone on affairs of the post office and where in April he was given another honorary degree at William and Mary; missed him there, was sent back to Philadelphia, and caught up with him in New York. In the meantime, Jane's daughter Sarah, not yet eighteen, was married in March to William Flagg, son of a Boston innkeeper. The young husband seems to have had no trade, and worked at manual labor.

Franklin's reply from New York, written late in June, teased his sister a little for her "extravagant thanks" but told her all he knew about her restless son. The original agreement between Franklin and Benny, the letter explained, had been that the nephew, like his predecessor, was to pay one-third of the profits of the Antigua press to his uncle, who was to furnish the capital and all the initial expenses. But after a year or so, when the Blue Ball had been sold and the Mecoms had moved into their "dearer" house, Franklin, finding Benny "diligent and careful," told him that if he would pay his mother part of her rent and another small sum to his uncle in sugar and rum for his family use, he could have all the rest to himself. "I cannot remember what the whole of both payments amounted to, but I think they did not exceed twenty pounds a year." Franklin's intentions from the first were to give Benny the printing house outright, and to turn back all the money received into new types. "I thought it best not to do it immediately, but to keep him a little dependent for a time, to check the flighty unsettledness of temper which on several occasions he had discovered. . . .

"This proposal of paying you and me a certain annual sum," Jane read on, "did not please him; and he wrote to desire I would explicitly tell him how long that annual payment was to continue; whether on payment of that all prior demands I had against him for the arrears of our first agreement were likewise cancelled; and finally insisted that I would name a certain sum that I would take for the printing house, and allow him to pay it off in parts as he could, and then the yearly payments to cease; for though he had a high esteem for me, yet he loved freedom, and his spirit could not bear dependence on any man though he were the best man living."

The letter in which Benny declared his independence reached Philadelphia, Franklin went on to say, when he was off on one of his long journeys of the momentous year 1755, and could not be answered as soon as Benny expected. Benny took offense, and without waiting for an answer wrote again, announcing that "he had come to a resolution to remove from that island; that his resolution was fixed, and nothing that could be said to him should move or shake it; and proposed another person to me to carry on the business in his room. This was immediately followed by another and a third letter to the same purpose, all declaring the inflexibility of his determination to leave the island; but without saying where he proposed to go or what were his motives." Franklin, he explained to his sister, did not care to continue the Antigua arrangement with a third partner, and wrote to Benny to ask that the press there be either sold or else shipped back to Philadelphia. Benny might leave the island if he chose. "I shall be very glad to hear he does better in another place, but I fear he will not for some years be cured of his fickleness and get fixed to any purpose. However, we must hope for the best, as with this fault he has many good qualities and virtues."

Neither Franklin nor his sister could yet understand that Benny's fickleness was the premonitory symptom of a progressive mental disorder which got fitfully worse throughout the twenty years he had yet to live. Because of his disorder and his shocking end, all his letters except a few to Deborah Franklin were destroyed after his death, and most of the family letters that mentioned him, except certain of his uncle's to his mother which she preserved. She thought them the best and truest record of the story, and there is no reason to think she was in error.

Benny returned from Antigua to Philadelphia later in 1756, and arrived in Boston early in the following January, riding a horse his uncle had lent him for the journey. "He has settled accounts with me," his mother read in a letter he brought from his uncle, "and paid the balance honorably. He has also cleared the old printing house to himself, and sent it to Boston, where he purposes to set up his business, together with bookselling, which, considering his honesty and frugality [that is, if he is honest and frugal], I make no doubt will answer. He has good credit and some money in England, and I have helped him by lending him a little more; so that he may expect a cargo of books and a quantity of new letter [type] in the spring; and I shall from time to time furnish him with paper."

What Jane did not read, because her brother did not tell her, was that Benny still owed his uncle a hundred pounds, and that he had settled "honorably" by signing a bond for the amount with the condition that if he paid half of it within a year the whole indebtedness would be discharged. When he sold the borrowed horse in Boston for half what it was worth, Franklin would accept no more. And in a new will made the following April he bequeathed Benny the unpaid bond—which of course was never paid and is still among the Franklin papers.

Benjamin Mecom, himself a trouble-breeder, found trouble already breeding in Boston, on account of his brother Peter. After the death of his uncle John Franklin, Peter was unable to get on with the widow and her children, who were after all his aunt and cousins only by marriage. He left the house in Cornhill and found employment with some other soap-boiler, who was already making crown soap or, perhaps, began to make it with the benefit of Peter's experience with his uncle. In the November of the year John Franklin died his widow notified the public in the *News-Letter* "that there are sundry persons endeavoring to impose on people a sort of soap which *they call* crown soap, which a little resembles it in appearance, but is vastly unlike it in quality, by which the character of the soap has suffered greatly with some persons who have not taken particular notice: the papers [wrappers] being so nearly the same as easily to deceive; and there never was in New England any person but the late Mr. *John Franklin* that made the true sort of CROWN SOAP. It is now carried on by Mrs. *Elizabeth Franklin* at the post office in Boston."

The Mecoms, who could not yet be aware that Peter was showing the first signs of a mental disorder even worse than his brother Benjamin's, took Peter's side in the quarrel, in which both families were soon involved. Benjamin, once more in Boston, brought up a fresh grievance. John Franklin had been succeeded as postmaster by his stepson Tuthill Hubbart. Was it proper for that Franklin office to go to a step-nephew of the postmaster general, when there was a blood nephew who deserved, and needed, it more?

Jane Mecom, with her "miffy temper" and her ailing husband from whom she could not expect such prudent counsel as her brother was used to giving her, appealed to Franklin in unusually frequent letters, all now lost. She told him that Benny had taken a house in Cornhill, nearly opposite the First Church and near the Town House, where he was to sell books and install his printing press as soon as it arrived. Moreover, he hoped to marry Elizabeth Ross, of Elizabeth, New Jersey, whom he had met probably while he was still with James Parker in New York and had seen on his recent journey from Philadelphia to Boston. For the time being Jane's printer son seemed as full of promising schemes as his uncle had been at the same age, and it was not yet clear that the nephew hopelessly lacked his uncle's judgment.

From other sources it appears that Benny, living up to his uncle's present fame, refused to be the plain tradesman his uncle had been at the outset of his career. Whereas Benjamin Franklin in his early days at Philadelphia had made a point of now and then bringing home paper to his shop in a wheelbarrow, to show that he was not above his business, Benjamin Mecom, helping at another printer's press while he waited for his own, wore "a powdered bob wig, ruffles, and gloves: gentlemanlike appendages which the printers of that day did not assume. . . . He indeed put on an apron to save his clothes from blacking, and guarded his ruffles; but he wore his coat, his wig, his hat, and his gloves, while working at the press."

Peter Mecom too had crowding ambitions, and thought of putting the Franklin coat of arms on the wrappers of his crown soap, as his uncle had done. Of the other sons, Edward was in bad health, Ebenezer was planning to open a bakery of his own, John was a good and diligent workman, and Josiah of course was still learning the saddler's trade from his father.

And there was the matter of Elizabeth Douse for Jane to consult her brother about. Their eldest sister was now eighty, a widow living in her run-down house in Unity Street, with a companion taking care of her. Might it not be better for the aged sister to sell her house and furniture and go somewhere to board, with perhaps less trouble and expense? Jane knew that her brother Benjamin was supporting Elizabeth, with money furnished her from time to time by yet another nephew as Franklin's agent. This was Jonathan Williams, married to Grace, daughter of the dead sister Anne Harris.

Jane, writing three letters in hardly more than as many weeks for advice about her troubling problems, had a special reason in the spring of 1757. Franklin was in New York, waiting for the packet that was to take him to England as agent for the Pennsylvania Assembly. There was danger the ship might be captured by a French cruiser or privateer; and in any case he would be long absent and too far away for her to count on prompt replies.

His three surviving replies, out of the four he wrote her in April and May, are the only mirror in which she can be seen during those anxious weeks. But it is easy to imagine her, waiting for his letters in the house near the Orange Tree, and being guided and comforted by what she read as they came.

First about Elizabeth Douse. "As having their own way," Jane read, "is one of the greatest comforts of life to old people, I think their friends should endeavour to accommodate them in that as well as in any thing else. When they have long lived in a house, it becomes natural to them; they are almost as closely connected with it as the tortoise with his shell; they die if you tear them out of it. Old folks and old trees, if you remove them, 'tis ten to one that you kill them. So let our good old sister be no more importuned on that head. We are growing old fast ourselves, and shall expect the same kind of indulgencies. If we give them, we shall have a right to receive them in our turn.

"And as to her few fine things, I think she is in the right not to sell them, and for the reason she gives, that they will fetch but little. When that little is spent, they would be no farther use to her; but perhaps the expectation of possessing them at her death may make that person"—her companion—"tender and careful of her, and helpful to her, to the amount of ten times their value. If so, they are put to the best use they possibly can be.

"I hope you visit Sister as often as your affairs will permit, and afford her what assistance and comfort you can, in her present situation. Old age, infirmities, and poverty, joined, are afflictions enough; the neglect and slight of friends and near relations should never be added. People in her circumstances are apt to suspect this sometimes without cause; ap-

pearances should therefore be attended to, in our conduct towards them, as well as realities.

"I write by this post to Cousin Williams to continue his care,
which I doubt not he will do." Jonathan Williams' care, Jane
knew, would include the payment of her brother's money for
Elizabeth Douse's living expenses.

Then about Benny's courtship of Elizabeth Ross. "I know
nothing of that affair but what you write me, except that I
think Miss Betsey a very agreeable, sweet-tempered, good
girl, who has had a housewifely education and will make, to
a good husband, a very good wife. Your sister"—that is,
Deborah Franklin—"and I have a great esteem for her, and
if she will be kind enough to accept of our nephew, we think
it will be his own fault if he is not as happy as the married
state can make him. The family is a respectable one, but
whether there be any fortune I know not; and as you do not
inquire about this particular, I suppose you think with me
that where everything else desirable is to be met with, that is
not very material. If she does not *bring* a fortune, she will
help to *make* one. . . . We can only add that, if the young
lady and her friends are willing, we give our consent heartily,
and our blessing."

There was a postscript, in a handwriting less skillful than
Jane's, from Deborah Franklin, who had come from Philadelphia to keep her husband company while he waited for his
sailing. "If Benny will promise to be one of the tenderest hus-
bands in the world, I give my consent. He knows already what
I think of Miss Betsey."

As to Jane Mecom's sons, there was little her brother could
say about three of them. He hoped that Edward would "get
over the disorder he complains of, and in time wear it out."
Franklin was pleased to hear that Ebenezer was "likely to

get into business at his trade. If he will be industrious and frugal, 'tis ten to one but he gets rich, for he seems to have spirit and activity." John must remember that if he ever set up as a goldsmith, he could not possibly thrive unless he had a reputation for perfect honesty. "It is a business that, though ever so uprightly managed, is always liable to suspicion; and if a man is once detected in the slightest fraud, it soon becomes public, and every one is put upon his guard against him; no one will venture to try his wares or trust him to make up his plate; so at once he is ruined."

About the troubling Peter and Benjamin, Jane found, her brother was more detailed. "I am glad that Peter is acquainted with the crown soap business, so as to make what is good of the kind. I hope he will always take care to make it faithfully, and never slight the manufacture, or attempt to deceive by appearances. Then he may boldly put his name and mark [on it], and in a little time it will acquire as good a character as that made by his late uncle, or any other person whatever" —such as, Jane reflected, his late uncle's widow. "I believe his aunt in Philadelphia [Deborah Franklin] can help him to sell a good deal of it; and I doubt not of her doing everything in her power to promote his interest in that way. Let a box be sent to her (but not unless it be right good), and she will immediately return the ready money for it. It was beginning once to be a vogue in Philadelphia, but Brother John sent me one box, of ordinary sort, which checked its progress. I would not have him [Peter] put the Franklin arms on it; but the soapboilers' arms he has a right to use, if he sees fit. The other would look too much like an attempt to counterfeit" —to counterfeit, that is, the crown soap made by John Franklin's widow. "In his advertisements he may value himself on serving his time with the original maker"—John Franklin—

"but put his own mark or device on the papers, or anything he may be advised to as proper; only on the soap, as it is called by the name of crown soap, it seems necessary to use a stamp of that sort, and perhaps no soapboiler in the king's dominions has a better right to the crown than himself."

Jane could not miss the quiet insistence that Peter in his crown soap should avoid the inferior quality or the deceptive appearance against which Elizabeth Franklin's advertisement had warned the public; but that crown soap had always been marked with a crown, and Peter had as good a right as John Franklin's second wife to use the crown still.

"And now," Jane read on, "as to what you propose for Benny, I believe he may be, as you say, well enough qualified for it" —that is, the postmastership at Boston—"and when he appears to be settled, if a vacancy should happen it is very probable he may be thought of to supply it; but it is a rule with me not to remove any officer that behaves well, keeps regular accounts, and pays duly; and I think the rule is founded on reason and justice. I have not shown any backwardness to assist Benny, where it could be done without injuring another. But if my friends require of me to gratify not only their inclinations but their resentments, they expect too much of me. Above all things I dislike family quarrels, and when they happen among my relations nothing gives me more pain. If I were to set myself up as a judge of those subsisting between you and Brother's widow and children, how unqualified I must be, at this distance, to determine rightly, especially having heard but one side. They always treated me with friendly and affectionate regard; you have done the same. What can I say between you but that I wish you were reconciled, and that I will love that side best that is most ready to forgive and oblige the other? You will be angry with me here, for putting you and them too much upon a footing; but I shall nevertheless be, dear sister, your truly affectionate brother."

If Jane felt anger, she did not feel it long, and never for an instant toward her brother. But these were hard times for her, with her husband and her eldest son ill, and so many children growing up, and Benjamin and Peter willful and difficult. Of her brother's affection she had no doubt whatever. She would have been even surer of it if she had known the provision for her in the will he made while he waited in New York. "I give to my dear sister Jane Mecom the mortgage I have on my Sister Douse's house and lot in Boston, with said Douse's bond, and every demand I have against my said Sister Douse's estate. Only I will that my said Sister Douse be never disturbed in the possession of the said house and lot during her life, though she should not be able to discharge the said mortgage or pay the interest arising on the same. Also I give to my sister Jane Mecom the share of my father's estate and the particular legacy which he left me by his will, and also the debt due me from that estate." There were other bequests to kinsmen in New England, but Jane was still her brother's peculiar favorite, and she loved him as near idolatry as she ever came.

4

Sorrows Roll Upon Me

FOR more than forty-five years Jane Mecom had lived a life recorded almost wholly in the mirror of her brother's letters, with a few glimpses to be caught in the bare dates of births and deaths in her "Book of Ages," and random notices concerned with other members of her family. But on January 29, 1758, she spoke for herself, in the earliest of her own letters that survive. It was to Deborah Franklin, about a preposterous rumor suddenly, mysteriously spread in Boston. Franklin, the rumor said, had been made a baronet and appointed governor of Pennsylvania. Without doubting the truth of it, Jane breathlessly sent congratulations to Franklin's wife, in these words, with this spelling and punctuation: "Dear Sister

"for so I must call you come what will & If I dont Express my self proper you must Excuse it seeing I have not been acostomed to Pay my Complements to Governor and Baronets Ladys   I am in the midst of a grate Wash & Sarah still sick, & would gladly been Excused writing this Post but my husband says I must write & Give you Joy which we sinsearly Joyn in; I suppose it will not be news to you, but I will tell you how I [came] by it, Mr Fluker Tould Cosen Willams & he Doctor Perkins who Brought it to my Poor Son nedey who has a nother relapse into Raising Blood & has not Done won stroke of work this month but was Just a going to begin when he was again taken Ill pray Pardon my Bad writing & confused composure & acept it as coming from your Lady-ships affectionat Sister & most obedent Humble Servant

Jane Mecom."

It turned out that Franklin was neither baronet nor gover-nor, and Jane for two years wrote no letter that still exists. The year 1758 was full of zigzag fortunes. Her sister Lydia Scott died. Benny Mecom, who had married "that nice girl" Elizabeth Ross and brought her to Boston, seemed enterpris-ing and industrious. He was the first printer anywhere to undertake a separate printing of the famous Preface to *Poor Richard* for that year, called by Benny *Father Abraham's Speech* but later, in innumerable printings in many languages, *The Way to Wealth.* With it the ambitious nephew printed, for the first time, Franklin's drinking song "My Plain Country Joan," sung to the tune of "The Hounds Are All Out." In Au-gust came the first issue of Benjamin Mecom's *New-England Magazine* and its first printing of the Epitaph on the tomb-stone of Josiah and Abiah Franklin. In October Sarah, "daugh-ter of Elizabeth Mecom," was baptized at the Brattle Street Church, with no mention of the father's name. That same month Jane Mecom got a long letter from her brother in Lon-don.

"I wonder you have had no letter from me since my being in England. I have wrote you at least two, and I think a third, before this, and what was next to waiting on you in person, sent you my picture." He had seen the letter from Uncle Benjamin which when Jane was eleven had called her "a good humored child. So keep up to your character, and don't be angry when you have no letters." He wrote gaily and teas-ingly, and concluded: "My wife will let you see my letter

containing an account of our travels" the past summer, "which
I would have you read to Sister Douse, and give my love to
her. I have no thoughts of returning till next year, and then
may possibly have the pleasure of seeing you and yours—
take Boston in my way home."

With the hope of meeting, pain in parting came soon to
Hanover Street. Edward, the eldest son, died intestate in
December, at twenty-seven, leaving a widow and an infant
daughter named Jane after her grandmother. The fathers of
the young couple were joined with Ruth Mecom in the administration of the small estate. "E Mecom," Edward's father,
put his only known signature to the bond. Of the other sons,
Peter was still making crown soap in Boston, with what success does not appear. Ebenezer had opened a bakery in Cape
Ann (Gloucester) and was doing well. John, working at his
trade, made some silver spoons ordered by Deborah Franklin, who gave them to Benny and his wife for a wedding
present. The aunt in Philadelphia, who had never seen any
of the Mecom children except Benjamin, was kind to the
whole family. Benny, who was already in her debt and probably remained there, wrote her agreeable letters. She was Jane
Mecom's most regular correspondent in America.

From Franklin in England came letters about his travels,
and the English relative he had met, and in 1759 a small legacy
from the English Jane Franklin whose married name was
Fisher. In January 1760 he smiled again in a letter at his sister's
habit of taking humorous remarks seriously. Not that he
meant any reproof—"for if I were disposed to reprove you,
it should be for your only fault, that of supposing and spying
affronts, and catching at them where they are not. But as you
seem sensible for this yourself, I need not mention it; and as
it is a fault that carries with it its own sufficient punishment,

by the uneasiness and fretting it produces, I shall not add weight to it. Besides, I am sure your own good sense, joined to your natural good humor, will in time get the better of it."

With the letter came a new cloak for her. She had prudently decided against buying a cloak she wanted, she told him. He approved her prudence, but sent her a new cloak anyway. In the same letter he referred to the recent death of Elizabeth Douse, in October 1759. Of the thirteen Franklins that had grown up, "there now remains but three. As our number diminishes, let our affection to each other rather increase." Only she and Benjamin and their valetudinarian brother Peter in Newport were left.

In March 1760 Jane wrote again to Deborah, this time a letter with a characteristic variety of subjects. She was glad her brother was in good health in London, but wished he were coming home. She asked Deborah to send her a pamphlet published in Philadelphia on the tenure of judges—presumably for some friend in Boston who cared more about such things than Jane Mecom did. Then a paragraph about her family's health, here printed as she would have preferred it spelled and punctuated.

"Benny and Betsey are well with all their family, and our relations in general except poor little Jenny Mecom"—Edward's orphaned child—"who seems to be going the same way of her father and sister. She pines away and loses her appetite, but withal her bowels swells prodigiously so that with a little slip out of a chair she bust herself. She seems often to have something choking in her throat and don't incline to stir, but mostly keeps in her cradle. Her mother has but ill health—but why should I enumerate troubles? It is an unpleasing subject."

With resolute cheerfulness Jane spoke of an unidentified nephew of Deborah's named Benjamin. "Little Ben," Jane wrote, "has experienced what is the common fate of all children at some time or other; but the little rogues all want to be pitied by them that loves them; and I suppose to receive that comfort he would be brought to you to kiss the dear lip after it was hurt. If you please you may add to the number on my account who would have taken pleasure in an opportunity to do it myself. Does he look like his uncle?"

Poor little Jenny died, and her mother in November married another poor man, Thomas Foot, a cabinet-maker, who had lost most of his property in that year's disastrous fire. The year was for Benjamin Mecom, on the surface, the most active he spent in Boston. When he printed his uncle's Canada pamphlet, *The Interest of Great Britain*, of which the authorship had been a guarded secret in London, Benny took advantage of his relationship to the author and ascribed the work on the title page to "B——n F——n, LL. D." In February 1761 he wrote to Deborah Franklin about his new daughter, named Deborah "in grateful remembrance of the numerous kindnesses we have received from Mrs. Franklin. If our daughter proves as worthy a woman we shall be contented. Debby is put out to a reputable woman at Charlestown, at four shillings sterling per week. Betsey is weak yet, but has no milk, and parted with her child with great regret on that account." He told his aunt about the marriage of "Sister-in-law Ruthy" to Foot, "a joiner, who appears to be a sober, well-inclined, industrious husband, and we hope will be a continual comfort to poor brother Edward's valuable widow." The news about Peter Franklin Mecom was not so promising. He had returned from "the camp," to which he had apparently gone to enlist, or try to enlist, in the Massachusetts forces raised in 1760 for the attack on Canada. "Though he was unwell when he first came to town, he is now quite recovered, and thinks seriously of settling to business; nothing prevents his really doing so but *want*"—that is, wanting to. "We are unwilling to disturb you with our uneasiness, hoping hereafter to be able to send you better news."

Peter was in fact settling into the imbecility which within a year or so made him helpless and thereafter a constant charge for all his remaining years—boarded with a woman in the country, supported by Franklin, and unwittingly responsible for the later destruction of letters that mentioned him and consequently took with them into oblivion many facts about Jane Mecom and her family.

The loss of letters leaves the year 1761 blank in her bleak annals, but in January 1762 a fresh entry in the "Book of Ages" marked the beginning of five years for which the death entries provide the index.

"Janeuary the 18 1762 this morning Died a worthy & Dutiful Son Ebenezer Mecom."

Ebenezer had come back to Boston to die, probably in his mother's house, at twenty-seven like Edward—and like their sister Sarah two years later. There was no stamina in the best of the Mecom children. Years later Jane was to write her saddest words about her fate as mother: "I have had some children that seemed to be doing well till they were taken off by death." Ebenezer was one of these. Whatever his malady was, it left no name or symptom in the record. It may have been tuberculosis, like Edward's; or it may have been some taint in the Mecom blood which Jane referred to when after her husband's death she said he had "suffered much by sin and sorrow." His sin, or the sin of fathers or grandfathers visited upon him and his unstable, irresponsible, distracted sons?

She never said what it was, if she knew, and she blamed nobody—least of all God, whose justice she never permitted herself to question.

II

Ebenezer died in 1762; Peter grew steadily worse; and Benjamin suddenly gave up hope of making a success of his business in Boston, where he thought he had worked hard and knew he had lost money. When Franklin in November returned from England to Philadelphia, he found his namesake ahead of him, waiting for advice and help. Whatever the nephew got, he returned to Boston and moved to New York, where early the following year he set up his "Modern Printing-Office" in Hunter's Key, "vulgarly called Rotten Row." His brother John, restless too, went with him, and probably worked there as journeyman for some master jeweler.

Franklin, welcomed with eager letters from both his sister Jane and his young friend Catharine Ray, who was Mrs. William Greene and living at Warwick, Rhode Island, told them both that he would visit New England the coming year, and of course would see them. His son William, married in London, came back to be royal governor of New Jersey—even if his father was not governor of Pennsylvania. But Franklin was still postmaster general, and must make a survey of the whole American postal system from Virginia to New Hampshire.

About the first of March Jane received a letter from her brother with an exciting inquiry. "Tell me how you do, and where you live, and what you would advise me to do concerning lodging when I come to Boston. As I think I shall stay two or three months, I have half a mind to keep house, that is, bachelor's hall, in that which was Sister Douse's. Cannot one hire furniture for a quarter or a half a year? In London one may very easily." Jane replied, in a missing letter, with an invitation to Franklin to bring his wife and daughter, and to lodge with the Mecoms. In June she got another letter from him, now in New York on his way to New England. "I purpose to lodge at your house if you can conveniently receive me." He could not persuade his wife to undertake the journey, but he hoped to bring his daughter Sarah, who would be twenty that summer. "If you cannot accommodate us both, one of us may lodge at Cousin Williams's—on second thoughts, it will be best that she should be there, as there is a harpsichord, and I would not have her lose her practice; and then I shall be more with my dear sister."

On July 20 Franklin and his daughter, traveling in a chaise with an extra saddle horse which the two took turns in riding, arrived at the boarding house in Hanover Street. They were full of talk about the long trip: of John Foxcroft, Franklin's new colleague in the post office, who had traveled with them; of Franklin's fall from the chaise or the saddle and his bruised chest; of the too-brief visit at Catharine Greene's house with her husband and children.

Peter Franklin had come from Newport, perhaps with his brother and niece, and was in Boston for a few days of happy reunion. Peter soon returned to Rhode Island, Sally settled into Jonathan Williams' house with the harpsichord, and her father and Foxcroft went off on their postal business as far as Portsmouth, New Hampshire. At Portsmouth Franklin had another fall which dislocated his right shoulder, so that he could hold neither whip nor reins. Once more in Boston, he had to "lie by a while" with Jane Mecom, the most tender of nurses, and a little too solicitous.

Her household was now smaller than it had been the last

time Franklin visited her. Two sons were dead and two in New York. Peter Mecom was helpless, perhaps already sent off to the country. Sarah was married and lived elsewhere with her four children. Josiah was at home, working in the saddler's shop which saw little of his wasted father. The two younger daughters were infirm and languishing victims of the obscure Mecom malady. And there was a new lodger, Sarah Davenport Bowles, who was a stepdaughter of Jane Mecom's dead sister Sarah. After the death of Sarah Bowles' husband, an apothecary, she had come to her step-aunt's inexpensive boarding house to live. The Mecoms, under obligation to James Davenport for teaching their son Ebenezer his trade of baker, could not refuse to oblige Davenport's widowed daughter.

In this depressing household Franklin made himself as much at home as if he were in his own comfortable house in Philadelphia or in the still more comfortable one in Craven Street where he had lived during his five happy years in London. The "constant though not very acute" pain in his shoulder never made him irritable toward his solicitous, worshiping, touchy sister. He learned what he had perhaps not fully known before—the facts about her son Peter—and proposed to Jane a method of supporting him. There was Elizabeth Douse's house which had come to Franklin on a mortgage. That could be rented, and the rent be used for the "maintenance of her unhappy son," as Franklin described it to Jonathan Williams. In this case she must have forced from her brother, or from "Cousin Williams," the details of the transaction. Elizabeth Douse at her death owed her brother, for money advanced, a little over two hundred and fifty pounds. Her house was appraised at a hundred pounds less. As it was badly in need of repairs, he had to spend almost a hundred and fifty pounds more to make it suitable for a good tenant and a sufficient rent. Jane, anxious economist, could not help seeing that her brother had invested in the house nearly three times what it was worth, and yet was letting her have all the income. As prices then went in the country near Boston, the rent of fifteen or so pounds a year would pay some farmer's wife to give Peter all the care he knew enough to need or wish.

Quiet as Franklin was about his benefactions to his family, Jane noted them and kept them in her memory. There was their niece Dorcas, daughter of their sister Sarah, who had married a man named Stickney ("who never loved work" according to Jane) and lived in poverty in Newburyport. Franklin visited them on his way to Portsmouth and made them "a handsome present." Edward Mecom's widow Ruth was still poor, and Franklin commissioned her new husband, Thomas Foot, to make a sticcado, a kind of xylophone, and probably also a chair and a case for an armonica, the musical instrument lately devised in London by Franklin himself.

Jane was happy over her brother's concern with music during this visit. They went to Jonathan Williams' house near the Drawbridge in Ann Street to hear Sally Franklin play on the harpsichord. Josiah Williams was a promising young musician, already skillful on the instrument. The members of the two households, visiting back and forth, formed a lasting attachment. Grace, Jonathan's wife, was or became Jane's favorite among her Boston nieces. Jonathan, in whose hands Franklin now settled his Boston affairs, was the most dependable of their nephews, though he was a nephew only by marriage. As Franklin's agent, Williams learned about Jane Mecom's difficulties. From this year on he took the place almost of a son to her—now that she had only one son left in Boston, Josiah the saddler, who like his brothers was becoming restless and intractable, with thoughts of the sea that had drawn his uncle Josiah Franklin off to long voyages and his death.

If Franklin had known that this was the last time he would ever see Boston and most of his relations there, neither he nor Jane could have planned his visit better. His accident prolonged his stay and confined him a good deal to her house. She was hostess to a famous man, disposed to make her own favorites among her nieces and nephews especially welcome: the more agreeable Homeses; Mary Davenport and her husband John Rogers; Abiah Davenport and her husband John Griffith. There were cousins from Nantucket, salty and gruff in the metropolis. It was not so pleasant for Jane to watch her step-niece Elizabeth Hubbart coquette worshipfully with the philosopher, and hear her call him her "dear Papa" and hear him call her his "dear Child." One member of Betsey Hubbart's circle who came with her to call was Benjamin Kent. He seemed to Franklin to practice a kind of harmless inverted hypocrisy, pretending to be worse than he was.

Of course Jane Mecom's physician, John Perkins, and her minister, Samuel Cooper, paid their respects. Then there were other clergymen: Jonathan Mayhew of the West Church, powerful in his pulpit on political themes and stout for liberty; Mather Byles of the Hollis Street Church, a poet, easygoing, and loyal to the royal government, as he was to remain through the Revolution. Byles and Franklin, almost the same age, had known each other in childhood, perhaps had been pupils together in the Latin School; and they were affectionate friends now as through life. Franklin's young friend James Bowdoin and Professor John Winthrop from Harvard came to talk science as well as politics. Franklin, who spoke slowly and little, was an incomparable cause of conversation in others, whom he guided or followed from theme to theme,

the master of the discourse. All her life after this visit Jane
missed the "suitable conversation" which she felt she had
known at its best only then and one time later, again with her
brother.

On October 13 Franklin and his daughter left Boston for
Philadelphia, visiting his countless friends as they went. In
Newport he arranged that his brother Peter should give up
his store and his ship and move to Philadelphia as postmaster
there. In the second of Franklin's letters back to Jane, which
she received about the end of December, he told her: "Brother
Peter is with me, and very well, except being touched a little
in his head with something of *the Doctor*"—that is, practic-
ing medicine on himself—"of which I hope to cure him. For
my own part, I find myself at present quite clear of pain,
and so have at length left off the cold bath"—which had been
part of his own treatment in Hanover Street. "There is however still some weakness in my shoulder, though much stronger
than when I left Boston, and mending. I am otherwise very
happy in being at home"—and here he began to tease his
sister—"where I am allowed to know when I have eat enough
and drank enough, am warm enough, and sit in a place that
I like, etc., and nobody pretends to know what I feel better
than I do myself." Then, before she could be too much hurt:
"Don't imagine that I am a whit the less sensible of the kindness I experienced among my friends in New England. I am
very thankful for it, and shall always retain a grateful remembrance of it. Remember me affectionately to all that inquire
after, Dear Sister, your loving brother." And a postscript:
"My compliments to good Mrs. Bowles. Sally writes."

In February he sent a dozen prints of his portrait to Jonathan Williams to be given to Boston friends who had called
in Hanover Street, and perhaps asked for pictures: the three

clergymen, Bowdoin and Winthrop and Kent, Betsey Hub-
bart, and the "cousins" Rogers, Griffith, Williams. "And my
Sister will possibly like to have one for herself, and for her
Doctor Perkins."

III

With 1764 Franklin entered the busiest three or four years
he had ever lived, deep in the stormy politics of Pennsylvania
and the struggle over the Stamp Act. For Jane Mecom these
were years of more anxiety and loss than even she had ever
known. Her son Benjamin, after only a year in New York,
failed again in business, and moved now to New Haven, where
his uncle had a printing press and where the nephew was commissioned deputy postmaster. His brother John remained for
the time being in New York, no more disposed than Benny
to keep their mother regularly informed about what they were
doing or how they were making out.

To her uncertainty about them was added grief at home.
"June the 12–1764," she wrote in her "Book of Ages," "Died
a beloved & Deservedly Lamented Daughter Sarah Flagg.
She has left four children, Jane mary Josiah & Sarah."

From Philadelphia came the most comforting words that
Jane could have read in her bereavement. Sarah Flagg, Franklin said, had been "of a sweet and amiable temper" and had
"many other good qualities that must make the loss of her
more grievous for Brother and you to bear. Our only comfort
under such afflictions is that God knows what is best for us
and can bring good out of what appears evil. She is doubtless
happy—which none of us are while in this life." In another
letter he explained that his wife and Peter Franklin had re-
frained from writing to her in order to save her the cost of
postage, which she would have had to pay. Jane saw nothing

trivial in this excuse. The cost of sending a letter written on a single sheet from Philadelphia to Boston was about forty cents, paid by the recipient; and forty cents in Jane Mecom's money was the price of a pair of shoes. A new postal regulation made it unlawful for Franklin to frank letters, if by others, not on official business. He could not violate the trust, and Jane could not afford to pay avoidable postage.

The widowed William Flagg and his children came to live with the Mecoms in Hanover Street; and soon there were further entries in the "Book of Ages":

"Novr 9–1764 Died under my Care my Daughter flaggs youngest Child [Sarah] aged 17 months.

March 1765 bigining Died my Daughter Flagg second Daugter Polly a sober Plesent Child."

Their brother Josiah had a fall in some unexplained accident and injured his knee so badly that, with no more medical attention than he got, he was crippled for life. A letter from Jane Mecom to Deborah Franklin in April 1765 was largely a bulletin of death and sickness. Polly Mecom "holds better but far from well. The sick child I mentioned to you in my last"—Polly Flagg—"died the next day, and the other child's knee grows worse." The father's arm, apparently hurt at the same time with Josiah's knee, "grows better, but is so weak he cannot lift it to his head nor do the least thing; and my Sarah"—the old servant—"has kept her bed ever since except two or three days she has sat up in a chair about two hours, so that my mind is kept in [such] a continual agitation that I don't know how to write."

Close upon these bad fortunes came worse: "Sepr. 11–1756. God sees meet to follow me with Repeeted corrections this morning 3 oclock Died my husband in a Stedy hope of a happy hear after"

Seventeen days later the widow wrote again to Deborah Franklin. "Nothing but trouble can you hear from me, but I do my endeavor to adopt the great Pope's doctrine with regard to the Providence of God: 'Whatever is, is right.' In fifteen months I have been bereaved of four near and dear relations. In a few days after I wrote my last to you it pleased God to call my husband out of this troublesome world where he had enjoyed little and suffered much by sin and sorrow. He is gone to a world of spirits from whence none has ever returned to give us an account of what is there transacted, but it has pleased God to favor us with a revelation in which we are assured the godly shall enjoy a perfect happiness in His presence forever.

"Mr. [Samuel] Cooper"—now minister at Brattle Street —"the first Sabbath I went to meeting after a long confinement with my sick family comforted me with a sermon from the fourth chapter of Second of Corinthians, 17th verse: 'For our light affliction, which is but for a moment, worketh for us a far more exceeding and eternal weight of glory.' He shew in how many respects afflictions worked thus to a believer, and only to them; for to the wicked worldly sorrow worked death; and that it was Paul that could say this that had met with such a large portion of affliction ever since he professed Christ. To me the sermon was a masterpiece of the kind, and several others I heard speak of it were of my mind. But I am not good at repeating or remembering, though I hope I retain so much of the sense as in some measure to enable me with the assistance of God's spirit to influence my conduct here in this world and through the merits of Christ give me hopes of a glorious eternity."

Edward Mecom died intestate. His widow, administering the estate, was joined with her son Josiah, as a matter of form, and her nephew Jonathan, who was her real security for the bond she was required to make. Appraisers came to the boarding house in October and valued all the furniture, the equipment of the shop, and Edward Mecom's clothes ("1 Thick Sett Coat 2 old Coats &c 1 Bever hat 1 old hat 2 old wigs") at £41.6.4. Jane paid £4.12 for funeral charges and five pounds to "her Doctor Perkins" for his care in the last sickness. The remainder of the estate was allowed to her "for necessary implements and her trouble as administratrix." The judge of probate was Lieutenant Governor Thomas Hutchinson, who treated the widow with a generous courtesy for which she could not say enough in gratitude and praise. This was the year of the Stamp Act, and a senseless mob had destroyed Hutchinson's house in Garden Court near enough to where the Mecoms lived for them to know of the uproar through the August night, with Edward Mecom on his deathbed.

Jane could afford no luxury of grief. Hardly was her husband dead when she took in two other relations to board. They were Elizabeth and Sarah, neither of them over fifteen, the daughters of Jane's dead niece Elizabeth Davenport and her husband Lieutenant Colonel Joseph Ingersoll. Ingersoll, who had served in the recent war, kept the Bunch of Grapes at the corner of King (now State) Street and Mackril Lane (now Kilby Street). It was a flourishing tavern, where Ingersoll that year was charged with unlawfully having a billiard table on the premises and where angry men were meeting to organize protests against the Stamp Act: no place for young girls to live. Better for them to be in the charge of their aunt Jane Mecom in quiet Hanover Street.

Franklin, in England again, seemed far away from Boston. Jane's first letter did not reach him at all; her second, now lost, found him still unaware that Edward Mecom had died. Her third, written on December 30, is the earliest of her surviving letters to her brother. She had been hurt by hearing from him so late about something he did not know; she was troubled by the abuse of him in America for naming his friend John Hughes to the post of stamp distributor in Philadelphia; and she was outraged by the violence shown to Governor Hutchinson and his house.

Still, she said, the letter which had at last arrived by way of Nantucket was "extremely comforting to me, as I was almost tempted to think you had forgot me; but I check these thoughts with the consideration of the difficulties you must labor under in the situation you are in in these difficult times. I can never forget that you have been not only the best of brothers but as a tender father to me and mine. So I have always a pleader in my own bosom that finds an excuse for all unkind appearances.

"There has never anything given me so great a shock on your account as to see your friend Hughes appointed stampmaster. I feared his appointment was by your means, but even this I concluded you must have some good reasons for, which others could not see into. The confusion and distress those oppressive acts have thrown us poor Americans into is undescribable by me, but you see the newspapers full of them. But they have fallen very short, I am told, of a [tragic?] description of the Lieutenant Governor's (Hutchinson) sufferings, which all circumstances considered was never equalled in any nation, Our Saviour's only excepted; and like Him I am told he bore it: praying for his enemies at the instant they were persecuting him. And our obdurate hearts will do nothing to make up his loss.

"He is now going from us, the greatest ornament of our

country, and the most indefatigable patriot. He does me the honor to be the bearer of this, and has shown me the greatest clemency in the capacity of a judge. May God protect and preserve him still for the good of mankind, and confer on him the honor he deserves. My writing so much of the Governor at this time looks as though influenced by his goodness to me in particular, but I assure you my opinion of the gentleman was the same before I had any business with him and my concern at the unjust treatment he met with [so great?] that for some days it overpowered all my other troubles (which were then very great). I think you and His Honor may compare notes and console one another."

As to her own affairs: "My family is now in a better state of health than they have been for two years past. Old Sarah lives yet and is got down stairs again.

"I have son Flagg boards with me, and Cousin Ingersoll's two daughters. Mrs. Bowles is also returned after a twelve-month's absence. But I have them all at a low rate because I can do no better; so that my income supplies us with victuals, firing, candles, and rent, but more it cannot, with all the prudence I am mistress of. But thus I must rub along till spring, when I must strive after some other way, but what at present I cannot tell, having no means for anything. I know my dear brother is always ready to assist the indigent and I now entreat your advice and direction [if] you think it proper to afford me it at this time, [and] endeavor it shall not be thrown away. I feel now as if I could carry on some business if I was in it; but at other times I fear my years are too advanced to do anything but jog on in the old track. But my two daughters, if they have their health, are capable and willing to do their part towards getting a living; and Son Flagg is dutiful and kind and takes much care off my mind, but he has two children to maintain and is in no way but his own hand labor.

"I have wrote and spelt this very badly, but as it is to one who I am sure will make all reasonable allowances for me and not let any one else see it, I shall venture to send it and subscribe myself your ever affectionate sister."

Then she remembered something she or he had formerly said about her writing, and added a postscript: "When I read this over I see so many 'buts' I am ashamed. Place them to the old account." And later: "This was wrote some time ago, but His Honor is still uncertain when he shall go and there is some things in this I want you should know. I send it by this opportunity"—that is, by John Williams, a brother of Jonathan.

Before Jane Mecom could receive her brother's reply to this, her old friend Captain Freeman arrived from London with presents from Franklin. "We are now," she wrote to Deborah Franklin in February, "supplied with not only necessary but cred[it]able clothing, for Brother has sent us each of us a printed cotton gown, a quilted coat, a bonnet; each of the girls a cap and some ribbons. Mine is very suitable for me to wear now, being black and purple cotton, but the girls' are light colored. . . . I have at present a competency and will not fear but it shall always be so. If I should now repine or distrust Providence I should be the most ungrateful of all His creatures; for I have been abundantly supplied beyond what I could rationally expect and [have] my two daughters in health: whom I had great reason to fear incurable, one of a painful disease, the other falling into a languishing. . . .

"I am amazed beyond measure at what Cousin Davenport tells me, that your house was threatened in the tumult" of anger against Franklin on account of the charge that he had favored and encouraged the Stamp Act. "I thought there had been none among you would proceed to such a length to persecute a man merely for being of the best of characters and really deserving good from the hand and tongue of all his fellow-creatures. I knew there was a party that did not approve his prosecuting the business he is gone to England upon, and that some had used him with scurrilous language in some printed papers; but I was in hopes it had so far subsided as not to give you any disturbance. When I think what you must have suffered at the time, how I pity you; but I think your indignation must have exceeded your fear. What a wretched world would this be if the vile of mankind had no laws to restrain them!"

Josiah Davenport, who had stood guard in Franklin's house when it was threatened, brought some money from Deborah and her kind greeting to the Mecom family. Jane sent her some domestic gossip in return. Her niece Abiah Griffith could "assign no cause for the death of her child except it was a fright she received one evening, her husband being absent when some men in liquor next door got to fighting and there was screaming murther." Grace Williams "looks soon to lie in. She is so big I tell her she will have two. Poor Sarah has been better so as to wash the dishes, but she is now worse again. Her age, as you say, is not a time to expect a cure for old disorders; and the doctor says there is no hopes for her, but she will dwindle away. She is a good creature, and patient. It would grieve you to hear what a cough she has that repels all medicines, but she is hardly ever heard to complain."

Franklin, who had not expected the Americans to resist the Stamp Act so vigorously as they did, had opposed it, and had been working tirelessly for the repeal which came in March

1766. In his reply to his sister, that month, he said about Edward Mecom only that he had been a "truly affectionate" husband to Jane, "and fully sensible of your merit." She was not to be disturbed at what was said about her brother and the Stamp Act. "I have often met with such treatment from people that I was all the while endeavoring to serve. At other times I have been extolled extravagantly where I have had little or no merit. These are the operations of nature. It sometimes is cloudy, it rains, it hails; again 'tis clear and pleasant, and the sun shines on us. Take one thing with another, and the world is a pretty good sort of world, and 'tis our duty to make the best of it and be thankful." Franklin used this occasion to tell his sister that Governor Francis Bernard of Massachusetts and Lieutenant Governor Hutchinson should not be accused in America of favoring the Stamp Act, when both had in fact advised against it. "Surely the New England people, when they are rightly informed, will do justice to these gentlemen and think of them as they deserve."

There is no way of knowing when Jane Mecom learned that her son John had been married, on the very day his father died, to Catherine Ouke of Brunswick (New Brunswick), New Jersey; or that he drifted with his bride to Philadelphia and lived on his aunt Deborah Franklin; or that he left Catherine there while he sailed to the West Indies on some unrecorded errand, saying he would send for her to follow him; or that he came back and moved on with his wife to Brunswick, where he again worked at his trade with what little energy and ambition his increasing malady allowed him. His mother made no mention of him in her surviving letters of these anxious years.

Grieved and harassed as she was, she kept her indomitable spirit. "You once told me, my dear brother," she wrote to

Franklin in November 1766, after their brother Peter had died in Philadelphia the past July, "that as our numbers of brethren and sisters lessened, the affections of those of us that remain should increase to each other. You and I only are now left. My affection for you has always been so great I see no room for increase, and you have manifested yours to me in such large measure that I have no reason to suspect its strength; and therefore know it will be agreeable to you to hear that myself and the children I have the care of"—the small Flaggs—"are in no worse situation than when I last wrote you."

She had of course read *The Examination of Doctor Benjamin Franklin* before the House of Commons, printed in England and reprinted throughout America, and she now reported to him: "Your answers to the Parliament are thought by the best judges to exceed all that has been wrote on the subject; and being given in the manner they were are a proof they proceeded from principle and sufficient to stop the mouths of all gainsayers." She had read an attack on him printed in Philadelphia: "a vile pretended letter which . . . gave me some uneasiness when I heard of it, before I could get a sight of it; and considering when a great deal of dirt is flung some is apt to stick. But when I read it I see it was filled with such barefaced falsehoods as confuted themselves. Their treatment of you among other things makes the world appear a miserable world to me, notwithstanding your good opinion of it. For would you think it, our General Court [Assembly] has set almost a fortnight chiefly on the subject of indemnifying the sufferers by the late mobs, and can't yet get a vote for it, though they sit late in the evening and the friends to it strive hard to get it accomplished. I have six good honest old souls"—as lodgers—"who come groaning home day by day at the stupidity of their brethren. I can't help interesting myself in the case, and feel in mere panics till they have brought the matter to a conclusion." (There is no record of the satisfaction she must have felt when the Assembly indemnified Hutchinson, or her opinion of the Assembly's raising the money by a lottery.)

"And," Jane turned away from politics to go on, "I have a small request to ask, though it is too trifling a thing for you to take care of. Mrs. Stevenson"—his landlady in Craven Street—"I don't doubt will be so good as to do it if you will give her the materials. It is to procure me some fine old linen or cambric (as a very old shirt or cambric handkerchiefs) dyed into bright colors such as red and green, a little blue, but chiefly red; for with all my art and good old Uncle Benjamin's memorandums I can't make them good colors." The reason for this request was that her daughter Jenny, with her mother's assistance, had become a milliner and was making artificial flowers "for the ladies' heads and bosoms, with pretty good acceptance. And if I can procure them colors I am in hopes we shall get something by it worth our pains, if we live till spring. It is no matter how old the linen is—I am afraid you never have any bad enough."

That same November Jane wrote also to Deborah Franklin, with more sharp-tongued gossip than she permitted herself to send her brother. Since the death of Peter Franklin, and of his wife a few weeks later, Deborah had sent Jane a box of clothes and books left by the dead. Jane, acknowledging them, had a story to tell about Ephraim Brown, adopted son of Peter and Mary Franklin, and a former maid in their household.

"You say you have heard nothing of the young man since he came from your place, but that he intends for England.

I heard that too, and that he came to Providence with the maid and his sister, and left the maid to come to Boston with the carrier, he and his sister coming the day before in a chaise, to go to Concord to visit his relations; and that the maid's own sister told at Providence that he and his sister was to wait for her at Boston and that she was to be married to him. I heard also that she gave the carrier a dollar extraordinary to bring her and half a dollar to tackle his chaise to bring her to my house and that the carrier should say she had a little trunk almost full of dollars; and I am sure she had a purple chintz gown on vastly finer than any gown I have in the world. My thought is that they two"—Brown and the maid—"pilfered all of all kinds that they thought you could not detect them in; for I am sure my brother and sister would not have left themselves so bare as it seemed. She [Mary Franklin] always kept herself full of good living, and I heard one say that saw her just before she left Rhode Island that she had very good shifts then by her that she had before she was married," in 1714, "and abundance of good aprons and handkerchiefs and laced caps, for they said she never wore a plain one. But perhaps these things are past recovery, as they two had all at their command when Sister was first taken and she not sensible [conscious], as the maid told me she was not. I asked her, 'how then could she give you so many things?' She said it was in their health they said she should have them. I said 'it was very odd they should give their own bed from under them in their health, when they did not know but you might die before them.' But after all their combinations I fancy he thinks himself too much of a gentleman to marry her, so she is wise, so far as that wisdom reaches, to keep her dollars to herself. He disappointed her with regard to visiting her in Boston, for they say he was gone when she got here and she

obliged to return with the carrier as she came. I have filled
the paper with such trumpery you will be vexed to give yourself the trouble of reading it, but as I han't time to write another must send it."

Margaret Stevenson, delighted to serve her American
friend's sister, selected the box of millinery goods which
Franklin sent to Boston by Captain Freeman. "They appear
to me to be extraordinary good of the kind," Jane wrote to
Mrs. Stevenson the following May; "and though the fashions
are new to most of us, I make no doubt they will obtain by
degrees when our top ladies set the example. . . . In the
meantime, if opportunity presents and any new fashion comes
out, of caps, or handkerchiefs, ruffles, aprons, cloaks, hats,
shades, or bonnets, and you will be kind enough to send me
patterns cut in paper with directions how to make them, and
how they are worn, it will add still greater obligations and
shall be gratefully acknowledged."

Politics interfered with Jane Mecom's pleasant plans to
increase her income by selling handsome accessories of English fashion to Boston's "top ladies." The new and unpopular
duties laid on importations to the colonies that year were
met by the colonists with a refusal to buy imported goods.
The refusal was strenuous in Boston. "It proves a little unlucky for me," Jane wrote her brother, "that our people have
taken it into their heads to be so excessive frugal at this time,
as you will see by the newspapers. Our blusterers must be
employed, and if they do no worse than persuade us to 'wear
our old clothes over again' "—here she was quoting the last
line of Franklin's *Examination*—"I can't disapprove of that
in my heart; though I should like to have those that do buy
and could afford it should buy what little I have to sell and
employ us to make it up."

If this was a disappointment, her son Benjamin's steady decline in New Haven was distress. He neglected all appeals to him to make his official accounting, kept the money received by him as postmaster, and in February 1767 was dismissed from his deputyship. He now had three more daughters, Abiah, Jane, and one whose name has not been found, with almost no income to support his family, and a stubborn confidence that his uncle would come back from England and be his patron in Philadelphia.

But this disappointment and this distress were nothing compared with Jane's agony over the event which she entered that year in her "Book of Ages": the last words she ever wrote in the sorrowful record.

"September 19–1767 at my Nantuckett at the House and under the most Affectionate care of my Dear Friend Kezia Coffin Died my Dear & Beloved Daughter Polly Mecom.

The Lord Giveth & the Lord taketh away oh may I never be so Rebelious as to Refuse Acquesing & & saying from my hart Blessed be the Name of the Lord."

Polly, nineteen, the youngest of the Mecom children then living, had gone to Nantucket to visit, or to live for a time, with Jane's friend Kezia Folger Coffin, one of the many Folger "cousins" on the island. Nantucket, Jane believed, was healthier than Boston. Kezia Coffin was well-to-do, and better able to care for the girl than her mother was. Yet death had found out the favorite daughter no matter where she went, and she was dead and buried before her mother heard the news.

Jane's heart cried out to her brother as never before in any of her griefs. "Sorrows roll upon me like the waves of the sea," she wrote in October. "I am hardly allowed time to fetch my breath. I am broken with breach upon breach, and I have now, in the first flow of my grief, been almost ready to say,

'What have I more?' But God forbid that I should indulge that thought, though I have lost another child. God is sovereign, and I submit." In December she wrote again. "Oh my brother, she was everything to me. Every word and every action was full of duty and respect, and I never looked upon her but with pleasure except when she was sick or in trouble. How to make me easy and happy was what she had most at heart; and rather than give me pain she concealed her own infirmities and did so much more than she was able that it increased her disorder and hastened her end."

Something undying in Jane, who would not doubt the justice of God or deny life even when she was tempted to ask "What have I more?" made her desire Franklin in her October letter to send her "all the pamphlets and papers that have been printed of your writing." Her brother replied in December with his wisest and tenderest sympathy for her loss, and then lightly changed his tone in speaking of her request.

"The longer we live," she read, "we are exposed to more of these strokes of Providence; but though we consider them as such, and know it is our duty to submit to the Divine Will, yet when it comes our turn to bear what so many millions before us have borne, and so many millions after us must bear, we are apt to think our case particularly hard, consolations however kindly administered seldom afford us any relief, natural affections will have their course, and time proves our best comforter. This I have experienced myself"—in the loss, Jane remembered, of his son Francis. "And as I know your good sense has suggested to you long before this time every argument, motive and circumstance that can tend in any degree to relieve your grief, I will not by repeating them renew it. . . .

"You desire me to send you all the political pieces I have been the author of. I have never kept them. They were most

of them written occasionally for transient purposes, and having done their business they die and are forgotten. I could as
easily make a collection for you of all the past parings of my
nails. But I will send you what I write hereafter, and I now
enclose you the last piece of mine that is printed. I wrote it
at a friend's house in the country who is of the Treasury, if
possible to do some service to the Treasury by putting a little
out of countenance the practice of encouraging smugglers in
buying their commodities. But I suppose it did very little."

On Jane Mecom the paper *On Smuggling* had so much effect that when, seven years later, she fled from beleagured
Boston and carried out some goods for sale packed among her
"wearing apparel, linen, and bedding," she conscientiously explained to her brother that "this was not an unlawful smuggling which you would have reproved, for they were not owed
for, nor any one cheated of duties."

5

Bad Weather Does Not Last Always

FOR the seven years after the shattering death of Polly Mecom only two letters from Jane Mecom to her brother and four to Deborah Franklin have survived accidental loss or deliberate destruction. Again for a time Jane was, in effect, almost silent about the seedy, crumbling fortunes of her sons. Letters from other Franklins have to tell the story. In May 1768 Deborah wrote to her husband: "I don't know whether you have been told that Cousin Benny Mecom and his lovely wife and five daughters is come here to live and work journey work," that is, as a hired not a master printer. "I had them to dine and drink tea yesterday. They have a little girl, a servant, so the company was eight in all. You used to love Betsey as I did. I could wish she had better luck." Franklin replied: "I cannot comprehend how so very sluggish a creature as Ben Mecom is grown can maintain in Philadelphia so large a family. I hope they do not hang upon you: for really as we grow old we shall find we have nothing to spare." Franklin's income had recently fallen off to about half what he was used to, and he was obliged to caution his wife about her spending.

William Franklin somewhat later wrote to his father in

more detail. "Cousin Ben Mecom is starving at Philadelphia and would have been, I suppose, in jail [for debt] by this time if it had not been for the assistance my mother and I have afforded him and his family. Goddard would have given 35 shillings a week to him if he would have worked as other journeymen do, but he insisted on coming and going just as he pleased, on which Goddard and he quarreled and parted. He has likewise been at work at some printing offices in Philadelphia, but cannot agree with anybody, and is I believe now without any employ. His pride and laziness are beyond anything I ever knew, and he seems determined rather to sink than to strike a stroke to keep his head above water. He has had seventeen pounds of me, and what of my mother I know not. He has got it into his head that you intend to set him up in a printing office on your return, and therefore seems determined to idle away his time till your arrival. In short, I look upon him to have a tincture of madness.

"I have likewise assisted his brother John with money, who has turned out as bad as Ben and gone and quartered himself and wife on his mother in Boston.

"I sometimes hear from Aunt Mecom, and have sent her some barrels of flour at different times, for which she is always very thankful. She lives better than ever, I am told, since her husband's death, and I expect her here on a visit in the spring if you return."

Not a surviving word from Jane Mecom to her brother about Benny; or about John except her bare statement in November that he and his wife were with her and sent "their duty"; and not a word about her son Josiah, who had left her, or was soon to leave her, to go to sea on a whaling vessel.

Instead, she spoke in her November letter about the public conflicts in which she had plainly not yet chosen sides. "The

whole conversation of this place turns upon politics and religious controversies, both managed with too much bitterness
—as you will see by the newspapers if you give yourself the
trouble to read them. But they will not infallibly inform you
of the truth; for everything that any designing person has a
mind to propagate is stuffed into them, and it is difficult to
know whether either party are in the right. For my part, I
wish we had let strife alone, before it was meddled with, and
followed things that make for peace. . . . I hope your endeavors for the good of the nation and the colonies will be
blessed with success and we shall at last be favored with quiet-
ness at least."

Franklin, replying in February to this and two missing letters from her, was pleased that she approved of Richard
Bache, who had married Sarah Franklin and brought her to
Boston to visit her relations there. Jane's occasional lodger,
Captain Ledlie, had written to Franklin about the proposed
new road between Hartford and Boston, but Franklin could
not say much on the subject till he had consulted with his
colleague Foxcroft. "I am glad Major [John] Small," a British
officer then with his regiment in America, "called on you. He
is a man I much esteem, as I do his brother"—Alexander Small,
a British Army surgeon—"with whom I am intimately acquainted here." As to the controversies in America, Franklin
did not object to the political ones, if "carried on with tolerable decency," but he disliked the religious squabbles. "When
religious people quarrel about religion, or hungry people
about their victuals, it looks as if they had not much of either
among them." His sister had sent no fresh orders for goods,
but Mrs. Stevenson was ready to oblige her at any time.
Franklin had already discharged his sister's debt to his landlady for goods previously shipped. The amount she sent by

Captain Timothy Folger of Nantucket she might now look upon "as so much of yours in her hands, and order in it what you please."

In a postscript: "There has lately been a new edition of my Philosophical Papers here": the famous 1769 collection of his *Experiments and Observations on Electricity made at Philadelphia in America. . . . To which are added, Letters and Papers on Philosophical Subjects.* "I send six copies to you, which I desire you would take care to have delivered as directed. There is one for your trouble." Two of the copies were for James Bowdoin and John Winthrop, who had called on Franklin at his sister's house, and one for Harvard College. The copy sent to her is the only book actually hers which is known to be still in existence, in a mutilated state, with "Mrs. Jane Mecom Her Book No. 11" boldly written in her hand on the half-title.

In January 1769 she wrote, it appears, that she heard he was to be an under-secretary of state in the British government. He replied in April that he was too old to be "ambitious of such a station," which would not be offered to him and which he would never ask for. "But even if it were offered, I certainly could not accept it, to act under such instructions as I know must be given with it"—that is, under instructions to carry out measures contrary to American interests. "The account you write of the growing industry, frugality, and good sense of my countrywomen gives me more pleasure than you can imagine: for from thence I presage great advantages to our country. I should be sorry that you are engaged in a business [in millinery and accessories] which happens not to coincide with the general interest, if you did not acquaint me that you are now near the end of it."

In September he replied to a June letter from her which he

had found waiting in London on his return from a visit to France. "It pleases me," he wrote, "to hear you are at present relieved from the weight which lately lay so heavy upon you that 'all the assistance of reason and religion were scarce sufficient to keep your spirits up.' It is well you had such aids. Our reason would still be of more use to us, if it could enable us to *prevent* the evils it can hardly enable us to *bear*. But in that it is so deficient, and in other things so often misleads us, that I have sometimes been almost tempted to wish we had been furnished with a good sensible instinct instead of it."

What particular crushing weight had been so heavy upon her can be no more than guessed at, but in that September there was a considerable change in her circumstances. Her son John and his wife had returned to her people in Brunswick; Josiah had gone to sea; William Flagg had married again and taken his children away from the boarding house. And Jane Mecom, leaving her daughter Jenny with some unnamed related family in Boston, was resolved to take the first long journey of her life.

"I have no letter from you," she wrote on the fourteenth to Deborah Franklin, "nor my son [Benny] since I wrote you I was going to Philadelphia, but still persist in my intent and purpose to sit out in about a fortnight, but shall stop a little at Brunswick and at Burlington and make them a longer visit at my return. I was in hopes to have had the company of your friend Mr. Hughes, but he talks not of going till November, which will be so late I shall not dare to venture. All other matters and things I shall leave to discourse on when I shall have the pleasure to converse with you by your own fireside."

John Hughes, now collector of customs and in Boston on the business of his office, was so much taken with Jane Mecom when he first met her that he felt obliged to justify his conduct in a letter to Deborah Franklin written five days after Jane's. "Upon my arrival at Boston I did myself the pleasure to wait upon your Sister Mecom; and although I am not very forward in saluting ladies, yet it was not in my power to refrain taking the sister of my good friend in my arms and saluting her. Perhaps the good lady may think that, as a stranger, I have been rather rude. And as I expect you will have the pleasure of seeing her this fall before I shall, I beg you will excuse me to the good lady, if any part of my conduct has been thought too free. But at the same time I must confess that it would be laying a great constraint upon my temper not to act in the same manner, was I to meet with another sister of Dr. Franklin's."

No other woman in America, then undertaking so long a journey alone, would have been more sure of friendship on the way than Benjamin Franklin's sister. Her brother's friends were planted along the road like milestones. Every postmaster, every post rider, every ferryman whose boat took the mails across a river, every innkeeper, would be her friend. Catharine Greene in Rhode Island was already her own friend, and Jane no doubt stopped at Warwick. She probably followed the main post road to New York, probably riding in a chaise (a one-horse, two-wheeled vehicle with a top) or a chair (the same without the top) under escort of the post rider for each stage. At New York she would be welcomed by Franklin's partner and Benny's former master, James Parker, and must visit him at his house in Woodbridge, New Jersey. Then she would go on to Brunswick, where John Mecom lived with his wife Catherine, called Catey by her family. From there to Burlington, to the handsome official residence of Governor William Franklin in Water Street, looking across the Delaware. In the manner of the time, William probably went in his carriage to meet his aunt, perhaps all the way to Brunswick, and he may have accompanied her to Philadelphia. All this is again without a syllable of record, till in October Deborah Franklin wrote her husband that "Antey Mecom" was expected soon in Burlington. On December 13 Deborah could report that "Sister is very agreeable to me and makes everything very pleasant to me, and we are as happy as we could expect to as in your absence, but we hope you will be as soon in the spring"—her words wandering as she wrote.

Deborah Franklin's house in Market Street was not so cheerful as it seemed to Jane Mecom, accustomed to the harassed boarding house in Boston. Deborah, whom Jane now saw for the first time, was infirm beyond her years, bothered with spells of dizziness and forgetfulness, lonely in the long absence of her husband whom she expected back each year, only to be disappointed. The house in Philadelphia could not be itself while the master was away. But Deborah and Jane talked and talked about Franklin; and there was his small grandson Benjamin Franklin Bache, four months old when Jane arrived. His grandmother called him Kingbird, and his great-aunt liked the name.

It was strange for Jane to go over her brother's house, so full of evidences of his planning and his taste, and to realize that he himself had never seen it. It was flattering to find so many of his friends eager to welcome her, whether or not any other was so demonstrative as his friend John Hughes had been in Boston. Thomas Yorke, who had served with Franklin in the Pennsylvania Assembly, was particularly "obliging" to Franklin's sister. The eminent Dr. Thomas Bond came to call. Jane went to hear Jacob Duché preach at Christ Church, which Deborah and the Baches attended. Without household cares on her shoulders, Jane could take some ease and have as good conversation as she could expect without her brother present. In January she wrote to tell him how agreeable she found her visit. He replied in March: "Since your family is so much reduced, I do not see why you might not as well continue there, if you like the place equally with Boston. It would be a pleasure to me to have you near me; but your own discretion must govern you."

There was a dark side to the picture of Philadelphia. Benny Mecom now had a printing press, his uncle's, shipped from New Haven and set up in a house in Arch Street, where the sluggish nephew lived with his charming, distressed wife and daughters, supported in part by Deborah Franklin's generosity. He had again failed at working for himself, and was soon to apply for a license to sell "spirituous liquors by small measure"—an application that was disallowed. There was nothing to do but go back to journey work for William Goddard, publisher of the *Pennsylvania Chronicle*. Benny's "pride and laziness" were diseases. And his brother John, Jane Mecom heard from Catey Mecom in Brunswick, was in as bad a state. There was no real hope for the Mecom sons.

To make these troubles worse, she fell, some time that winter or spring, down the stone steps that led to the garden at her brother's house, and was so badly hurt she was lame for months. But, for reasons not clear, she left Philadelphia, made her long way home, and wrote from there to her brother early in July. "You had not, I hope," he said in acknowledging her letter, "any offense in Philadelphia that induced you to leave it so soon." If she had taken offense, she never said so in any surviving letter, and her letters back to Deborah were full of happy reminiscences of the visit.

"Aunt Mecom is well settled in the old place, though almost

a new house," Jonathan Williams reported to Franklin in August. It was not the boarding house, but one nearer the Blue Ball, and in Hanover Street.

"I received your kind letter of June 25 some time ago," Jane wrote to Deborah in August, "but as I had just wrote to you (and enclosed it to Mr. Parker who I perceived by the papers was dead before that could reach him, yet I hope you have got it) and was in a hurry a-moving, I did not take the time to answer your letter, as I ought to have done; and one opportunity has slipped away after another, but you must forgive me, as you are sensible it cannot be for want of affection to you and your children, who are all very dear to me, but a variety of accidents happened to hinder me. . . . Your King Bird I long to see. I have watched every child to find some resemblance, but have seen but one, and that was only in good nature and sweet smell. . . . My lameness continues yet, [so] that it is with great pain I walk as far as Dr. Cooper's meeting. My daughter Jenny has been at home with me about a fortnight. She is well and sends her duty. I cannot git Jenny Flagg to live with me again. . . . Her father keeps her to tend his wife's children. . . . My son Josiah is not married. He is at sea whaling. I saw the woman. She is as comely, well-behaved a person as any you shall see in her station. She works for her living, and if they don't make themselves poorer by marrying I have no objection; for I am convinced poverty is entailed on my family—perhaps otherwise, and I endeavour to be content. Johnny has been sick ever since his wife wrote me to Philadelphia; has a bad cough, a chilly fit and fever every day, has not been able to do any work nor so much as write. His wife writes me he is pined to skin and bones. How is it with my son Ben and family? I should be glad to know. I have not got one letter since I came home."

John Mecom died the last day of September, and Jane did not mention him in her next surviving letter to Deborah, written about the end of the year.

"I received yours of the 15 inst. and you can't think how much pleasure it gave me to hear so particularly about the little grandson. I can't find one since I came home as looks a bit like him. I am glad you hear so often from my brother. I almost despaired when I wrote you last of ever having another letter from him; but soon after received one that by some means or other was four or five months a-coming. Several gentlemen arrived here from London says, as your Captain Sparks does, that he looks extremely well, and is in good health. . . .

"I have never yet recovered my fall, and cannot walk near so well as you can. . . . As I have now so good an opportunity I will endeavor to answer all your inquiries."

About her brother John Franklin's Hubbart stepchildren: Betsey, married for two years to Captain Samuel Partridge; Susannah, and Tuthill the postmaster. "In the first place, I have never seen Mrs. Partridge since I came home but once in the street. I have not heard whether she is like to have another child. The neighbors say she lay abed before with her hair powdered and a great plume in it. Suckey is not married. She once called to see me of an evening. I believe Tuthill has no thoughts of matrimony.

"Cousin Ingersoll has the same wife he had when Cousin Bache was here. I believe they are well. Their daughter was not like to have another child when I saw her last. . . . I have never heard whether Governor Wentworth [of New Hampshire] has a child. I see so few intelligent people that I know the least news of any one in the world. I am a great deal alone except some young persons coming back on errands; for as I

can't go abroad, people don't come to see me, and Jenny [her
daughter] is a good deal out.

"And now I have filled one side with answering your questions, give me leave to desire you to do the same by me—
even now before you forget it. You will find some opportunity
to send it. When do you expect Cousin Bache home?" Richard Bache had gone to England. "Is his wife like to have another child? How does Mrs. Smith's daughter and family do?
—if you will believe me I cannot now think of her name. How
is Dr. Bond and family? Do you ever see my obliging Mr.
Yorke? . . . Is it that Dr. [John] Shippen that is dead whose
child made the speech at your house? How goes on Goddard
and his sister? Did they ever pay my son the money they owed
him, or did you ever get your rent. . . . How does . . . Duke
of Wharton, Marquis of Rockingham? Did he ever get his
government?" This was Jane's pleasant way of asking about
Samuel Wharton, associated with Franklin in plans to found
a new western colony of which it was rumored that Wharton
might be royal governor. "How do you like Mr. Foxcroft's
lady?" This was Judith Osgood, whom John Foxcroft had
married in England and brought home to Philadelphia. "Is
Tommy [Thomas Foxcroft, postmaster of Philadelphia] married? Is Cousin All turned merchant and [to] stay at home
constantly? I have never seen him entered or cleared in the
papers." This was Captain Isaac All, a relative of Deborah
Franklin, who lodged in a house near hers. "I wish I had such
a constant boarder to pay me three dollars a week the year
round. I could then do pretty well.

"I am glad the child has his old maid. Tell her I always
think of her with respect. She was so good to me when I hurt
myself. Does George, Bob, and Jack do any better; and how
does the little mulatto behave to his master? Does Mr. Duché

preach as well as ever? I should admire to come and see and hear all about everything there once a year and stay a fortnight. I fancy so short a time would affect my health with change of climate. . . .

"Cousin [Sarah] Bache knows she is a letter in my debt, and I will not excuse her except she is in circumstances and very sick. So you must tell me that and everything that you know I shall like to hear. If you send it to my son [Benny], he will find a vessel to send it by. Please to tell them (my son and his wife) that I shall expect a long letter from each of them, for I have heard nothing of them this whole winter. I believe by this time you are heartily tired with this trumpery." And in a postscript: "Dear Sister, if Catey [John Mecom's widow] should send a letter to you for me, do be so good as git it sent to me by water."

In September of that year Jane Mecom wrote her brother the last surviving letter before a gap of four years. It was taken to London by two sons of Jonathan Williams, Jonathan Jr. and Josiah, sent there for training under Franklin's eye and guidance. The young Jonathan had business in mind, but Josiah had set his heart on studying music with John Stanley, the famous blind organist of the Inner Temple, who was Franklin's friend.

"Josiah," Jane wrote, "says he fears nothing he shall have to encounter so much as your disapprobation of his scheme. He expects you will advise him to return in the first ship, yet he can't conquer his inclination. I tell him you have seen so much of the follies of human nature and so little else in the common run of mankind that you will know better how to pity and advise him." She had heard a rumor that Franklin had been dismissed from his place in the post office on account of a letter he had written to Philadelphia, and it confirmed her

own bad opinion of the world in general. "I fancy by this
time you have found there are more wicked folks in the world
than you thought there was; and that they are capable of doing hurt. I pray God to preserve your useful life among
them and that every good man may not be destroyed from off
the face of the earth."

II

Then for four years she appears again almost wholly in the
mirror of his letters, which comforted and cheered her, and
confided in her more than in any other period of his life.

Josiah Williams, Franklin wrote late in December, "has at-
tained his heart's desire, of being under the tuition of Mr.
Stanley, who, though he had long left teaching, kindly un-
dertook at my request to instruct him, and is much pleased
with his quickness of apprehension and the progress he
makes; and Jonathan appears a very valuable young man,
sober, regular, and inclined to industry and frugality, which
are promising signs of success in business. I am very happy
in their company"—with him in Mrs. Stevenson's house in
Craven Street. Jane probably found out sooner or later from
the young men's father that they were supported by Franklin
in London to offset the money laid out by Jonathan Williams, Sr., in providing for her son Peter.

In these four years Jane Mecom had a chance to read first,
in letters then written for her eye and heart alone, passage
after passage that has since become classic to the world.

Of being deprived of his post because he had written letters
home, Franklin explained, he had at present no fear. His
friends defended him, and his enemies could do no more than
abuse him in the newspapers, hoping to provoke him to re-

sign. "In this they are not likely to succeed, I being deficient in that Christian virtue of resignation. If they would have my office, they must take it.

"I have heard of some great man, whose rule it was, with regard to offices, *never to ask for them, and never to refuse them;* to which I have always added, in my own practice, *never to resign them.*" He had served the post office in "inferior degrees" for years before he became postmaster-general; and when he assumed that rank the North American postal establishment did not earn enough to pay his salary. He had been "chiefly instrumental in bringing it to its present flourishing condition" and therefore thought he had "some kind of right to it. . . . As to the letters complained of, it is true I did write them, and they were written in compliance with another duty, that to my country: a duty quite distinct from that of postmaster. . . .

"Possibly they may still change their minds, and remove me; but no apprehension of that sort will, I trust, make the least alteration in my political conduct. My rule, in which I have always found satisfaction, is never to turn aside in public affairs through views of private interest; but to go straight forward in doing what seems to me right at the time, leaving the consequences with Providence."

In a letter of July 1771 he said: "You seem so sensible of your error in so hastily suspecting me"—of what is not known —"that I am now in my turn sorry I took notice of it. Let us then suppose that account balanced and settled, and think no more of it. . . . I meant no more by saying mankind were devils to one another than that, being in general superior to the malice of other creatures, they were not so much tormented by them as by themselves. Upon the whole I am much disposed to like the world as I find it, and to doubt my own judgment as to what would mend it. I see so much wisdom in what I understand of its creation and government that I suspect equal wisdom may be in what I do not understand: and thence have perhaps as much trust in God as the most pious Christian.

"I am very happy that a good understanding continues between you and the Philadelphia folks." He spoke of the "disputes and misunderstandings" between their father and Uncle Benjamin in those far-off days at the Blue Ball. "But you have been more prudent, and restrained that 'aptness' you say you have to 'interfere in other people's economical affairs by putting in a word now and then unasked.' And so all's well that ends well.

"I thought you had mentioned in one of your letters a desire to have spectacles of some sort sent you; but I cannot find such a letter. However I send you a pair of every size glasses from 1 to 13." And then Jane read a paragraph which countless ophthalmologists have read since. "To suit yourself, take . out a pair at a time, and hold one of the glasses first against one eye, and then against the other, looking on some small print. If the first pair suits neither eye, put them up again before you open a second. Thus you will keep them from mixing. By trying and comparing at your leisure, you may find out those that are best for you, which you cannot well do in a shop, where for want of time and care people often take such as strain their eyes and hurt them. I advise your trying each of your eyes separately, because few people's eyes are fellows, and almost everybody in reading or working uses one eye principally, the other being dimmer or perhaps fitter for distant objects, and thence it happens that the spectacles whose glasses are fellows suit sometimes that eye which before was not used, though they do not suit the other. When you have suited yourself, keep the higher numbers for future use as your eyes may grow older; and oblige your friends with the others." When Jane had finished this letter she knew virtually all that was then known about the choice and use of spectacles.

Then about another Sally Franklin, great-granddaughter of "our father's brother John," who had lived in Craven Street for the past five years and was now sixteen. Franklin had brought her there to give her an education that her father, a dyer like his father and grandfather, could not afford. "Having mentioned so many dyers in our family, I will, now it's in my mind, request of you a full and particular receipt for dyeing worsted of that beautiful red which you learnt of our mother. And also a receipt for making crown soap. Let it be very exact in the smallest particulars. Enclosed I send you a receipt for making soft soap in the sun." In a postscript: "I have mislaid the soap receipt, but will send it when I find it."

In August of that year John Foxcroft and his wife were in Boston. Jonathan Williams on August 5 reported to Franklin: "Aunt Mecom dined with us a few days ago with a large company, Mr. Foxcroft and his lady, etc." And Jane early in September wrote Deborah Franklin: "I am well, have got so far over my lameness as to be able to walk much about as well as I could before I fell, but you know that was but poorly, as you could outwalk me by a great deal. We shall neither of us now I believe attain to what my brother writes me of himself, that he has lately walked ten miles without resting, and is in fine health, which I am sure you and I join in blessing God for. Mrs. Foxcroft and myself have often pleased ourselves with talking of little King Bird. She agrees with me that he is an extraordinary fine child. . . . I love every one I had any acquaintance with at Philadelphia."

That fall Jane Mecom wrote out the receipt, now lost, for dyeing worsted red, and another receipt "For making Crown Soap" which, mislaid for many years, has recently been identified and printed. She may have copied it from an account, also now lost, written by her brother John, the inventor of the soap, or she may have reported the process from her own memory and experience. Carefully and circumstantially she told how to set the leaches; draw off the lye when it was "strong enough to bear an egg"; put in "clean hard tallow" and the "purest bayberry wax of a lively green color"; separate the mixture by sprinkling salt in it till the soap was "as clear as Madeira wine"; and so on, detail by detail of boiling and skimming and cooling and cutting and stamping it. Crown soap, the only invention by any Franklin besides Benjamin, owes to Jane Mecom the sole known record of how it was made.

In January 1772 Franklin thanked her for the receipts. "They are as full and particular as one could wish. . . . I am glad . . . that those useful arts, which have so long been in our family, are now put down in writing. Some future branch may be the better for it. . . .

"All who have seen my grandson agree with you in his being an uncommonly fine boy: which brings often to my mind the idea of my son Franky, though dead thirty-six years, whom I have seldom since seen equalled in everything, and whom to this day I cannot remember without a sigh."

In the same letter Franklin told his sister that he meant to force payment from a debtor in Boston who for seven years had failed to pay either principal or interest: "like a whimsical man in Pennsylvania, of whom it was said that, it being against his principle to pay interest, and against his interest to pay the principal, he paid neither one nor the other."

The laggard debtor was another nephew, Samuel Hall, a printer who had married one of James Franklin's daughters in Newport, and was now printer of the *Essex Gazette* in Salem. Jonathan Williams, in behalf of Franklin and with John Adams as attorney, brought suit against Hall in "July Court 1772." Hall paid a hundred pounds sterling the following January, and in delayed installments half as much again: in Massachusetts money a little over two hundred pounds. Franklin gave the whole amount to his sister, who had never in her life had so much at one time.

"Aunt Mecom wants to be doing," Jonathan Williams wrote to Franklin in February 1773. "She desires me to invest fifty pound of it in a bill of exchange and send it home to you, and she will accompany it with an invoice of such goods as she wants to make a beginning with. The remainder she wished to reserve there (if agreeable to you) as she thinks it may be improved [employed] to more advantage, and I believe it may." When the goods came in October Jane decided that she could in the future do better by buying wholesale from Boston importers, and so being sure that what she had to retail was suited to the tastes of her Boston customers. Then for almost two years she had capital, and a small stock, and neighbor women coming in to see her as well as her ribbons and laces, gauzes, chintzes, linens, cambrics, silks, ruffles, caps, sometimes shoes.

Moreover, Franklin that year made a present of fifty pounds for household furniture and equipment for Jane's daughter Jane, married in March to Captain Peter Collas. The younger Jane, now twenty-eight, thanked her "dear and Honored Uncle" with elegant raptures in a letter written in July. "My heart," she said, "has ever been susceptible of the warmest gratitude for your frequent benefactions to the whole of our family, but your last *kind,* unexpected as well as undeserved *noble* present in particular to me, calls for a particular acknowledgment from me. Accept then, dearest Sir, my most sincere and hearty thanks, with a promise that your kindness shall ever be gratefully remembered and your donation be made the best use of: as it will be laid out by my Mamma and the good Mrs. Williams, who is always ready, with Mr. Williams, to give their friendly advice and assistance on every occasion. Few are blessed with such friends as we are. How then can we be unhappy? I am not, nor would I change conditions with one person living, were I sure of fulfilling my most *ardent* wish: that every action of my life may be a credit to my Uncle. My constant endeavors and earnest prayers shall not be wanting. When, dear Sir, shall I have the happiness of thanking you in person for all your kindness? God send it may be soon. Till then, please to accept this incorrect scrawl and permit me to subscribe myself your sincerely affectionate, forever obliged, and ever dutiful niece, Jenny Mecom. P. S. The man who will share your goodness with me desires his most dutiful respects and sincere thanks."

Apparently this year saw also the beginning of a close friendship between Jane Mecom and her "poor little delicate neighbor" with whom she lived "so happily" for two years. Abigail Royall, daughter of William Tailler who had been lieutenant governor of Massachusetts, was the widow of Jacob Royall, who died in June, leaving his "large genteel brick dwelling house" in Orange Street mortgaged for more than it was worth. If Jane Mecom lived with Abigail Royall and her companion, Elizabeth Moncrieff, for two years, this seems to mean that the two lived with her as sole lodgers: which would mean less crowding, more regular payment, and better conversation. Jane barely mentions them, and Franklin never,

unless he had them in mind in February 1774 when he said
he rejoiced to hear of his sister's "welfare and easy situation."

In 1773 Jane Mecom wrote her brother more letters, all
missing, than usual: no doubt about Hall's money and the
arrangement with Abigail Royall, and certainly about Jane's
hope that Franklin would visit Boston that year. "1773 is my
period for visiting Boston," he said, "having left it in 1723,
and visited it in 1733, '43, '53, and '63." But politics kept him
in England, and she had nothing of him but his letters.

In a July letter she had a teasing compliment. "Is there not
a little affectation in your apology for the incorrectness of
your writing? Perhaps it is rather fishing for commendation.
You write better, in my opinion, than most American women.
Here indeed the ladies write generally with more elegance
than the gentlemen." And then a suggestion about the asthma
which had begun to trouble her. "Your shortness of breath
might perhaps be relieved by eating honey with your bread
instead of butter, at breakfast."

In an October letter he admitted sometimes failing to send
her things he had written, and now sent her his satirical *Rules
for reducing a Great Empire to a Small One*. The next month,
when she had wished he might be "a means of restoring harmony between the two countries," he explained his motive
in writing the *Rules* and the *Edict of the King of Prussia*. "I
had used all the smooth words I could muster, and I grew
tired of meekness when I saw it without effect. Of late therefore I have been saucy" and in those two papers had "held
up a looking glass in which some ministers may see their ugly
faces, and the nation its injustice. These papers have been
much taken notice of, many are pleased with them, and a few
very angry, who I am told will make me feel their resentment,
which I must bear as well as I can, and shall bear the better

if any public good is done, whatever the consequences to myself. In my own private concerns with mankind I have observed that to kick a little, when under imposition, has a good effect. A little sturdiness when superiors are much in the wrong, sometimes occasions consideration. And there is truth in the old saying, that *If you make yourself a sheep, the wolves will eat you.*" Here he added the caution: "This to yourself."

Resentments gathered against him, and at the end of January 1774 he was summarily dismissed from the post office. In February, when he had heard of her "easy situation" in Boston, he wrote: "You will hear before this comes to hand that I am deprived of my office. Don't let this give you any uneasiness. You and I have almost finished the journey of life; we are now but a little way from home, and have enough in our pockets to pay the post chaises. Intending to disgrace me, they have rather done me an honor. No failure of duty in my office is alleged against me. Such a fault I should have been ashamed of. But I am too much attached to the interests of America, and an opposer of the measures of administration. The displacing me therefore is a testimony of my being uncorrupted."

In May Jane wrote twice to her brother, and he replied reassuringly in July. "The report you mention that I offered to desert my constituents," the assemblies of Massachusetts, New Jersey, Pennsylvania, and Georgia for whom he acted as agent in London, "and banish myself" from America, "if I might continue in place, is an infamous falsehood, as you supposed. . . . They are every now and then reporting here that I am using means to get again into office. Perhaps they wish I would—but they may expect it till Doomsday. For God knows my heart, I would not accept the best office the king has to bestow, whilst such tyrannic measures are taking against

my country. Be assured I shall do nothing that will prejudice
me in your opinion, or be inconsistent with the honest public
character I have hitherto maintained. . . . They have done
me an honor by turning me out, and I will take care they shall
not disgrace me by putting me in again.

"All this to yourself. To the world such declarations might
seem incredible and a mere puffing of one's own character;
therefore, my dear sister, show this to nobody; I write it merely
for your satisfaction, and that you may not be disturbed by
such idle reports."

In September he renewed his assurances to her, already
sure of him and uplifted by his evident desire to have her ap-
proval. "I wish to know," he wrote, "how you fare in the
present distress of our dear country. I am apprehensive that
the letters between us, though very innocent ones, are intercepted. They might restore me yours at least, after reading
them; especially as I never complain of broken, patched-up
seals (of late very common), because I know not whom to fix
the fact on.

"I see in a Boston paper of August 18 an article expressing
'that it is now generally believed Dr. Franklin has received a
promise of being restored to the royal favor and promoted
to an office superior to that which he resigned.' I have made
no public answer to any of the abuses I have received in the
papers here, nor shall I to this. But as I am anxious to preserve
your good opinion, and as I know your sentiments and that
you must be much afflicted yourself, and even despise me, if
you thought me capable of accepting any office from this government while it is acting with so much hostility towards my
native country, I cannot miss this first opportunity of assur-
ing you that there is not the least foundation for such report;
that so far from having any promise of royal favor, I hear of

nothing but royal and ministerial displeasure. . . . I have seen no minister since January, nor had the least communication with them. The generous and noble friends of America in both Houses do indeed favor me, but they are in disgrace at Court as well as myself. Be satisfied, my dear sister, that I shall do nothing to lessen myself in your esteem or my own; I shall not with the least concurrence with the present measures merit any Court favor nor accept of any if it were offered me, which however is not at all likely to happen."

He had intended to return to America that year, but had now consented to remain till the proceedings of the First Continental Congress could be laid before Parliament; and he would not return till spring.

Jane Mecom had no natural bent to politics. The protest over the Stamp Act in Boston was for her, at first, chiefly a violent injustice done to Thomas Hutchinson, whom she liked as a man and whom in his sufferings she compared with her Savior. The non-importation agreements interfered with her little business. The continuing conflict she saw as disturbance of the peace. It took the various attacks on her brother to make her a patriot. The cause of Franklin was for her the cause of America, and her own.

Writing to him in November 1774, and acknowledging the pamphlet that told of his famous experiment on stilling waves by means of oil, she said: "I think it is not profanity to compare you to Our Blessed Saviour, Who employed much of His time while here on earth in doing good to the body as well as souls of men; and I am sure I think the comparison just, often, when I hear the calumny invented and thrown out against you while you are improving all your powers for the salvation of them very persons. Oh my dear brother, may you and I imitate Him also in holiness and in that way trust in Him for eternal happiness! I am well assured that you as well as myself are convinced that it must ever be imperfect here. . . . Not that I have met with anything new, for I am as happy as the present state of affairs will permit, owing to your bounty, without which I must have been distressed as much as many others.

"Dr. Chauncy," who was Charles Chauncy, minister of the First Church in Boston, "says we have already had miracles wrought in our favor; one of which is the uniting of the colonies in such a manner, another the extraordinary fruitful seasons and bounty of our friends," in other colonies which sent supplies to Boston after its port was closed by the royal government in retaliation for the Boston Tea Party. "But at present we have a melancholy prospect for this winter at least, the town's being so full of profligate soldiers," stationed there to keep order, "and many such officers. There is hardly four and twenty hours passes without some fray amongst them, and one can walk but a little way in the street without hearing their profane language.

"We were much surprised the other day upon hearing a tumult in the street; and looking out saw a soldier all bloody, damning his eyes but he would kill every inhabitant he met; and pressing into a shop opposite us with his bayonet drawn, bursting through the glass door; and the man of the house pushing him out; and he, to do what mischief he could, dashing the china and earthenware which stood on the window through the sashes with the most terrible imprecations. The case, it seems, was he perceived they sold liquor and went into the house demanding some; but being refused he went into the closet and took out a gun and said his commanding officer told him he might take anything out of the house he had a mind to. Upon which the battle ensued and the man

and his servant were both very much wounded. There were
two of them (soldiers), but I saw but one. A guard with an
officer came and carried him away, and I have heard nothing
of him since. But this has made me more timorous about what
may be before winter is out. My only comfort is, God reigns."

John Mecom's widow Catherine had been married, the past
June at New York, to Ensign Thomas Turner of the British
47th Regiment, and he was now in Boston. "He takes a great
deal of pains to convince us," Jane wrote, "he is a friend to
this country, having been here formerly and kindly treated.

"My daughter Collas has been in the country," in Roxbury,
"most of the summer and purposes to spend the winter
there, as she expects her husband will be most of the time at
sea. She has not courage to stay in town, and they have their
board so cheap, find it less expensive. She happened to be
here when I received your last, and desired her duty to you.
The man where she boards is the major of the regiment, and
is a moderate Whig, but can't be convinced that we ought not
to pay for the tea. . . . I think our Congress Address to the
People of England is a grand performance, and does them
honor, and shows there was really the wisdom among them
that the colonies endeavored to collect: which joined with
yours and the Bishop's"—she referred to Jonathan Shipley,
Bishop of St. Asaph, Franklin's friend and America's in the
conflict—"will I hope work some glorious effect. You have millions of prayers going up to heaven for it daily, private and
public.

"I have had no letter from Philadelphia a long time, though
I have wrote several times. The last I wrote I heard my sister
[Deborah Franklin] put under her cushion, I suppose in order
to read at more leisure, and perhaps never thought of it more,
and one of the children git it and tore it up. As we know, my

sister is very forgitful." As Jane did not know, Deborah was beyond reading or writing, and was within a month of her death
in December. "I think it is presuming on your patience," Jane
went on, "but I must just mention the horrid lie told and
published here about your son"—that is, that Governor William Franklin sided with the Crown against the Colonies. "At
first it struck [me] with a fear that it might be true, and I can't
express to you the pain it gave me on your account; but a little
consideration convinced me it was impossible, and I soon had
the pleasure of hearing it contradicted." But it was true, and
the breach between father and son was not far off. It was hard
for Jane to believe, for she had alway been fond of William,
and she loved his wife, and he was the son of her brother who
was her light and guide in the threatening struggle.

Franklin said nothing of this in the brief note which was the
last he ever wrote her from England, on February 26, 1775.
"I hope you continue well, as I do, Thanks to God. Be of good
courage. *Bad weather* does not last always in any country.
Supposing it may be agreeable to you, I send you a head"—
that is, a Wedgwood medallion portrait of him—"they make
here and sell in the china shops. My love to your children,
and to Cousin Williams and family. I am ever your affectionate
brother."

He was at sea on the day of Lexington and Concord.

My Dear Brother's Conversation

DURING the winter and spring before Lexington Jane
Mecom wrote her brother, she afterward told him, "a
great number of letters," but there is nothing to show that
they got to Craven Street. She believed they were intercepted,
and they may have been. Possibly some vigilant official in
London read her harmless domestic news. Benny Mecom and
his wife and five daughters, and a small son named John Ross
after his maternal grandfather, were in Burlington, where the
father could work a little at his trade in the printing house
of Isaac Collins, and hope for further help from Governor
Franklin since Deborah was dead. Josiah Mecom, Jane's sailor
son, was by spring home from his whaling. Her daughter Jane
Collas, whose husband was at sea, continued to board at Roxbury, partly because it was cheaper than keeping house in
Boston, and partly because she could be more leisurely and
ladylike in hired lodgings. Peter Mecom was still in his stag-
nant asylum in some farmer's house. William Flagg, living
in Boston with the dead Sarah Mecom's two children, and
his new wife, and her children, this winter "was taken in a fit
which terminated in distraction and confined him some time"
—as if the Mecom madness were catching. The note from
Franklin which told his sister that bad weather does not last
always in any country came to Boston in the ship with the

promising young Josiah Quincy, Jr., who had been trusted with the message and medallion for Franklin's sister, but himself died on the voyage home.

Such things were a sad old story to Jane Mecom, but calamity new to her followed the outbreak of April 19 and the bloody retreat of the British troops under fire from the muskets of the furious Americans. Whatever whispered rumor she may have heard of the British plan to seize the American military stores at Concord, she was not prepared for the uproar that it caused. Even her brother, she wrote him in May, could not imagine "the storm would have arisen so high as for the General [Thomas Gage] to have sent out a party to creep out in the night and slaughter our dear brethren for endeavoring to defend our own property. But God appeared for us and drove them back with much greater loss than they are willing to own. Their countenances as well as confession of many of them shew they were mistaken in the people they had to deal with; but the distress it has occasioned is past my description. The horror the town was in when the battle approached within hearing, expecting they would proceed quite into town; the commotion the town was in after the battle ceased, by the parties coming in bringing their wounded men, caused such an agitation I believe none had much sleep; since which we could have no quiet, as we understood our brethren without were determined to dispossess the town of the Regulars; and the General shutting up the town, not letting any pass out but through such great difficulties as were almost insupportable."

Never in its history had Boston known war close at hand. The inhabitants who could get away fled from the town as from a battlefield. Jane Mecom, infirm, asthmatic, had no man to turn to for counsel or assistance. Her nephew Jonathan

Williams, Sr., was away "at the time of the battle, and advised to keep out; and his poor wife slaved herself almost to death to pack up and secure what she could; and sent away her two daughters intending to go to him. And behold in comes he into town the day before I came out."

With desperate energy Jane Mecom managed to engage a wagon and load on it, she told her brother, "what I expected to have liberty to carry out, intending to seek my fortune with hundred others not knowing whither"; and just then came an invitation to her to take refuge with Catharine Greene in Rhode Island. "I brought out what I could pack up in trunks and chests," including "most of the things I had to sell," these tucked in among "our wearing apparel, linen, and bedding. . . . I wish I could have brought all my effects in the same manner, but the whole of my household furniture . . . I left behind, secured indeed in the house with locks and bars; but those who value not to deprive us of our lives will find a way to break through them if they are permitted." Jane Collas's effects, stored in her mother's house, also were left behind.

With her granddaughter Jane Flagg, "who I could not leave, if I had it would have been her death," and Abigail Royall and her family, Jane got past the lines at the Neck and to Cambridge where she was obliged to part with her delicate neighbor "in a most shocking disagreeable place." Then at a wagon's slow pace, over rough country roads, she traveled the rest of the forty-five miles to Providence, where Jane "had the unspeakable pleasure of hearing my dear brother was safe arrived at his own home." He arrived there on May 5, and she wrote from the Greene house at Warwick on the fourteenth.

"These people seem formed for hospitality," she told her brother, and "appear to be pleased with the vast addition to their family." In a solid farmhouse of eight rooms, with William and Catharine Greene and their five children, there were already ten refugees from Boston, including two children, a maid, and a Negro boy; and six more were expected the day Jane wrote. Most of them were related, at this or that cousinly remove, to the Greenes through the marriage of Catharine's sister Judith, now dead, to a stepson of John Franklin, Jane Mecom's brother. There were the wife of Thomas Leverett, bookseller in Cornhill, and two children and the maid, and three children yet to come. There were Susannah Hubbart and her sister Elizabeth, now Mrs. Partridge, whose attentions to Franklin Jane resented, and who did not much like Jane or the close bond between Jane and Catharine. But they had found a haven, and they lived happily in the fellowship of safety after peril.

"My own daughter," Jane told her brother in this first letter, "had been at board at Roxbury almost a year before, but she with the family were obliged to fly into the woods, and though they returned again they think themselves very unsafe; and she was in great concern what course to take, when the day before I left she received a letter from her husband that he was safe arrived at Bedford in Dartmouth"—New Bedford—"not daring to venture into Salem from whence they sailed. This also was a great ease to my mind, as she might now soon expect her husband to take the care of her." And in a postscript: "Dear Brother, I am told you will be joined to the Congress, and that they will remove to Connecticut. Will you permit me to come and see you there? Mrs. Greene says she will go with me."

From Catharine Greene another postscript: "Welcome, a hundred times welcome to our once happy land. Are you in health? . . . Your arrival gives new spring to all [I] have heard mention it. When shall we see you here? Do let it be

as soon as the Congress is adjourned, or don't know but your
good sister and self shall mount our old nags and come to see
you."

Franklin in Philadelphia, driven with new duties in Congress, did not till May 26 know where his sister was. Then,
learning from John Adams, also in Congress, that she was at
Warwick, he at once wrote: "I wish to hear from you, and to
know how you have left your affairs in Boston; and whether
it will be convenient for you to come hither, or you wish rather
that I should come to see you, if the business I am engaged in
will permit. Let me know if you want any assistance. . . .
Your very loving brother. . . . Send me what news you can
that is true." The country was filled with untrustworthy ru-
mors.

There was confusion in the post office, now suddenly taken
over by rebel hands, and this letter, plainly addressed in care
of William Greene at Warwick, went to Cambridge, then to
Newport, and lay there for three weeks before the postmaster
forwarded it to Jane Mecom on July 14, two days after she
received another from Franklin dated June 17—the day of
Bunker Hill, of which he did not hear till five days later.

Repeating his sympathy and offers of assistance, he said:
"I think so many people must be a great burthen to that hos-
pitable house; and I wish you to be otherwise provided for as
soon as possible; and I wish for the pleasure of your company; but I know not how long we may be allowed to remain
in quiet here if I stay here, nor how soon I may be ordered
from hence; nor how convenient or inconvenient it may be
for you to come hither, leaving your goods as I suppose you
have in Boston. My son tells me he has invited you to Amboy,"
where William Franklin had another official residence. "Perhaps that may be a retreat less liable to disturbance than

this: God only knows, but you must judge. Let me know however if I can render you any service, and in what way. You know it will give me pleasure. I hear that Cousin Williams is at last got out with his family. I shall be glad to hear from them, and would write if I knew where they were. . . . I am, thanks to God, very hearty and well, as is this whole family. The youngest boy"—William Bache now two years old—"is the strongest and stoutest child of his age that I have seen: he seems an infant Hercules." Franklin without explanation or comment told his sister what was perhaps the first she had ever heard of Temple Franklin, illegitimate son of Franklin's illegitimate son William. "I brought over a grandson with me, a fine lad of about fifteen. His father has taken him to Amboy. You will be pleased with him when you see him. Jonathan Williams," the younger, "was in France when I left London. Since I have been here I received a letter he sent me there. I enclose it for your amusement, and to show to his father and mother."

Replying on the day she got the second of these two letters from her brother, Jane reassured him: "Your care for me at this time, added to the innumerable instances of your goodness to me, gives me great comfort under the difficulties I feel with others; but not in a greater degree, for I am in want of nothing, having money sufficient to support me some time if I should go to board (which however Mrs. Greene will not consent to); and I have with me most of the things I had to sell and now and then sell some small matter." Jonathan Williams, Sr., and his family were in Worcester, in the house of the loyalist James Putnam, who had taken refuge inside Boston in the Williams' house. "My daughter Foot" had gone to Dunstable, "she in a bad state of health, left their goods in Boston." John Mecom's widow, now Catherine Turner, was in Boston with her husband. "How it has fared with them [I] cannot hear, though I wish them safe, for he really appeared a good sort of man. Oh how horrible is our situation, that relations seek the destruction of each other!"

Here Jane may have spoken with more pertinence than she knew. Ensign Turner's 47th Regiment was one of those that struggled up the cruel slope of Bunker (actually Breed's) Hill. Behind the breastwork was a detachment of Colonel Ebenezer Bridge's Massachusetts regiment, in which Jane's son Josiah had enlisted two weeks before the battle. If he was in the detachment which served that day, then her own relations or near-relations did seek to destroy each other.

More family news: "Poor Flagg, though he has used me very ill, I deplore his fate the more as there is two of my daughter's children left. I know not how they will be provided for." After Flagg's madness of the past winter, he "got so much better as to go about his business, and sent out his wife and children intending to follow them; but was soon after taken in the same manner as in the winter and died in a few days." His story, Jane said, was "too long and too full of shocking circumstances to trouble you with." His son Josiah, then fourteen and out of town, was later told that his father in June "came to his death by being poisoned while sick by a surgeon in the British Army by the name of Spencer who plundered the house of all its effects." Few things are less likely than this story, but it was one of the atrocities alleged by both sides against the enemy.

"My good Mrs. Royall and family that I lived so happily with two year is gone to Worcester. I have not received the invitation you say your [son] was so good as to send me nor a line from him a long time, though I have wrote several by such hands as I know he must have received. Cousin [Kezia]

Coffin has invited me to Nantucket. . . . I don't know if it would be prudent for me to go now." Jane was troubled at "being an encumbrance to this good family," but could not decide what course to take at present. "I wish you could advise me. . . .

"I could have wished you had been left to your own option to have assisted in public affairs, so as not to fatigue you too much; but as your talents are superior to most other men I can't help desiring your country should enjoy the benefit of them while you live; but can't bear the thought of your going back to England again, as has been suggested here and one sentence in your letter seems to favor. You positively must not go. You have served the public in that way beyond what any other man can boast, till you are now come to a good old age, and some younger man must now take that painful service upon them. Don't, pray don't go."

She had no news to send that she could be sure was true; "but my daughter wrote me last week from Roxbury that on our Army's firing cannon that reached into the fortification and killed six men, General Gage sent out word we had better not proceed to extremities, for the king had sent for two of the men-of-war home"—that is, had recalled two heavy armed ships to England, which Jane still instinctively called "home" as she always had.

Catharine Greene again added a postscript. Franklin, she said, must not fear his sister would "be troublesome" to her hosts. "Be assured that her company richly pays as she goes along, and we are very happy together, and shall not consent to spare her to anybody but her dear brother, was he to stay at home"—in America. "But if you are to journey we must have her, for she is my Mama and friend . . . and we divert one another charmingly. Do come and see us certain. Don't think of going home"—to England—"again. Do set down and enjoy the remainder of your days in peace." She sent her kind love to his family and signed herself his "affectionate friend as long as life."

Franklin, the oldest man in the Continental Congress, burdened by such labors as killed the younger Peyton Randolph, Simon Boerum, and Thomas Lynch within a year and a half, wrote his sister in August that the Baches thought she "had best come hither as soon as the heats are over, *i.e.* some time in September." After that she had no known communication with him till October, when he wrote her from Washington's Headquarters at Cambridge. He was there with two other delegates from Congress on the business of organizing the Continental Army. "I suppose we may stay here about a week," he told her. "In order to take you home with me, I purpose quitting their company, purchasing a carriage and horses and calling for you at good Mrs. Greene's. But let me hear from you in the meantime, and acquaint me with anything you would have me do or get towards the convenience of our journey."

The Greene house at Warwick, about ten miles south of Providence, when Franklin arrived had lost some of its refugees. The Leveretts had taken a house and set up a shop nearer the town. Most of the Boston cousins had found other refuge. Jane and Catharine had been free, late in the summer, to go to Worcester, to visit the Jonathan Williams and Royall families. Jenny Flagg, Jane's granddaughter, would be safe and happy with the Greenes. She was eighteen, skillful at spinning and sewing, and on the friendliest terms with Phebe Greene, three years younger. Leaving Jenny with the Greenes, Franklin would take their son Ray, ten, to Philadelphia to enter the Academy. Jane Mecom was now ready for the happiest journey of her life, on her last and longest visit with her brother, whom she had not seen for almost a dozen years.

They left Warwick about the end of the month, made recorded stops near Wethersfield and at New Haven and Perth Amboy, and were in Philadelphia about the middle of November. What the journey was like for Jane Mecom appears in a letter she sent back to Catharine Greene nearly a mouth after their parting. "My seat was exceeding easy and journey very pleasant. My dear brother's conversation was more than an equivalent to all the fine weather imaginable. But I met with one mortification on the road. We had appointed to dine at Wethersfield, where Mrs. [John] Hancock is, and had considerable talk about it. But we being engaged at that time in other conversation, the postillion drove us a mile or two beyond before we discovered it, and I could not prevail with him to go back, so we did not dine till we put up for the night."

The stop at Perth Amboy, at William Franklin's house, was tense, with Benjamin Franklin firm for the Americans in the conflict which had begun and his son still faithful to the royal government. Jane could not have been unaware of the tension, but in writing to Catharine she said only that the "house was very magnificent," and that they had let Ray see it "all over." In the short time since their arrival in Philadelphia the boy had caught the smallpox, a case so light that not more than ten pustules could be counted on his body. "I am afraid," Jane said cheerfully, reassuring his mother, "that he will not have one pit for a receipt. He has had no illness but one day a little shivery and feverish, so much as to say he was in no hurry for his coffee. We thought it not proper to make his clothes till we saw how it would fare with him, but now shall have them made with all expedition. He is very tractable, and here is a young gentleman"—Temple Franklin—"who sets him a complete example of good manners, that is, politeness. And my brother will give proper directions about his schooling. He will write himself as soon as he thinks it safe"—when there should be no danger of sending infection with his letter.

"I don't know that I got cold with my journey, but I have had a bad fit of asthma, am now as well as usual, have not had the colic, but do not sleep well on nights. Mrs. Bache is not yet abed"—with her third child. "She is as well as can be expected. I am so happy to have my choice of places of worship so near that the weather need not hinder me from going." Then in a postscript dated December 2: Some friend by whom she had hoped to send a parcel to Warwick had gone, "so Jenny must be without her silk till another opportunity. Ray is abroad and fine and hearty. Mrs. Bache was last night delivered of a fine girl," perhaps not yet given her name, which was Sarah.

In the first paragraph of this letter Jane Mecom put her bad news, and then no more of it. "Assure yourself the epithet of daughter which you seem to like to use cannot be disagreeable to me. Would to God I had such a one. All the allurements of this place should not separate me from her. I write not this in disparagement of my own daughter, for she is a good woman, but Providence does not permit us to be together. And as to sons, I have nothing but misery in those that are left." She had now heard that her son Benjamin was insane, like his brother Peter. "Both of them distracted, and I have heard of the death of poor Josiah since I came here, but by what means I am not informed." The records of Josiah's regiment show that his service expired early in August of that year. After that, no words about him but these in his mother's letter.

No wonder Catharine Greene wrote to Franklin in January: "My dear good friend your sister, is she not extreme low spirited for her? Dear lady, what continued scenes of misfortune she has waded through—enough to have buried several such as your friend."

II

Now for almost a year, except during April and May 1776 when Franklin was absent on the cold, unsuccessful mission to Canada, Jane Mecom was almost continuously in the same house with her brother, as close to the year's great events as any woman could be. Much of what he knew had to be secret till it could be published; nor is there any record of what she knew or thought or felt when she learned, from him or any other source, about the politics of Congress and the conduct of the war. She kept close at home, free to go to any church she chose on Sunday, and absorbed in the doings of the children in the Franklin household: the small Baches, Benjamin Franklin, William, and Sarah (who died in August 1776); the handsome Temple, brought up in London but now in the College his grandfather had founded in Philadelphia; and Ray Greene, who was Jane's special charge and who called her grandmother. She must have heard from time to time about her grandchildren in Burlington, Benny's daughters and son, but there is no record of it. She heard more often, it appears, about her granddaughter Jenny Flagg, with the Greenes in Rhode Island.

Jenny, a letter from Catharine Greene reported in January, was busy with her spinning and sewing. By February she had saved enough money to buy, Catharine hoped, a treasury note with interest at six per cent. "I wish you could get one with what you have got with you, unless you can do better with it." Jenny had gone to Coventry, Rhode Island, to help fit out the wife of Brigadier General Nathanael Greene so that she could accompany her husband to camp. "Jenny has two or three gowns to make here besides, and [I] think by the time she has done" at Coventry "she will be in a hurry to get home. We have had another killing lately, the spring pigs, and Jenny saw the whole process of it. She thinks she shall not love sausages any more; nor has she eat cheese since she saw what the rennet is made of"—the lining of calves' stomachs.

After the British evacuated Boston in March Jane heard that the goods left in her house there had been destroyed in the final days' looting by soldiers and sailors. Early in May two British ships of war came up the Delaware River toward Philadelphia and were engaged by American armed galleys in a sharp action which turned the invaders back. Jane Mecom, with her brother away in Canada, was almost determined "to set out for New England directly," she wrote to Catharine Greene; "and if I should I shall take Ray with me, for he would break his heart if I should leave him, and I have promised I will not. I cannot hear whether my daughter's goods are gone as well as mine, but expect they are; and I think there is but very little chance for her husband to escape being taken" with the ship he commanded. "She looks on herself already as a disconsolate widow, entreats me to promise her I will return, that we may live together." Jane Mecom was of a stouter temper. "What if I should go," she inquired of Catharine, "and take that house Mr. Leverett had near Providence, where I think we could get a living the way they began? I am afraid Boston is not sufficiently fortified yet"—against possible British attacks from the water.

Catharine Green, replying in June, insisted that the Leverett house was too "far out of town and from all your acquaintance. . . . I should by no means consent to your going there. You would not care to have the trouble of a horse, and it would be expensive hiring, and your business would be chiefly in town. If you do leave your dear brother I shall think myself happy to have you live with me. My regard for you is not of a summer's but from our first acquaintance." There was pleasant news about Jenny Flagg, who in a lost letter had told her grandmother of a young man the girl had met at Coventry and might marry. This was Elihu, one of the seven brothers of General Greene, who was a cousin of Catharine's husband. General Greene had asked Catharine if Elihu had consulted the William Greenes about his suit. "I told him no, but thought it was a civility due, and any want of respect to her [we] should resent as soon as [to] our own children. You may depend the girls don't tease her otherways than is agreeable in this case. We will forgive her, as it was her notion to find your sentiments," before asking the opinion of her hosts.

The Boston cousins, back home since the evacuation, had "particularly inquired after" the household goods Jane had left behind. "Some are in one place and some in another," but she must not expect to recover them all.

In June came as bitter an event as any in Franklin's whole life. The New Jersey Assembly ordered the arrest of Governor William Franklin for his resistance to the insurgent authorities, and put him under guard at his farm near Burlington. Congress on the twenty-fourth, when Franklin may have been present, resolved that the Governor should be sent from New Jersey to be interned in safer Connecticut. "He is son to Dr. Benjamin Franklin, the *Pennsylvania Evening Post* said, "the genius of the day, and the great patron of American liberty." In Burlington a Franklin nephew, Josiah Davenport, pre-

sented the Assembly with a bill for three pounds for boarding
the Governor and his servant for a week. Perhaps Josiah would
be considerate of his cousin William. But what could either
Benjamin Franklin or his sister say to the other?

July was the month of the Declaration of Independence.
July was the month in which two prominent citizens of Burlington wrote to Franklin at the request of Elizabeth Mecom,
"who has been an inhabitant of this city for some time past
and behaved with prudence and industry . . . to inform you
that her husband's conduct is such as to render her situation
disagreeable, and at times very dangerous, he being often
deprived of his reason and likely to become very troublesome
to the inhabitants. If a place in the hospital of Philadelphia
can be procured or any other way of confining which may
be thought more eligible, she begs your assistance and that
you would be pleased to favor us with an answer on the subject of this letter." Franklin, with so much else on his mind
and hands, arranged for the confinement and support of another mad nephew, in Burlington; and his sister, long past
hoping, gave up her last hope for any son of hers.

About the end of that month the William Greenes arrived
in Philadelphia, Greene on business for his state, and Catharine accompanying him to visit her best friends. Since the
three correspondents, Franklin, Jane, and Catharine, were
now for six weeks in the same house, there was no excuse for
letters, and for that time there is no record of Jane Mecom's
life. William Greene had the smallpox by inoculation, and
was soon as well as ever. On the day of their departure Franklin was at a session of Congress and could not take leave—
the last leave, it turned out—of his "friend as long as life."
Catharine, writing back, sent her love to his "dear sister . . .
whose heart is so divided between so good a brother and a

distressed daughter that, though she appears cheerful, [she] is very unhappy and for fear of making her friends so, keeps all to herself."

Jane was anxious about her brother because he was being sent by Congress as commissioner from the United States to France. He was past seventy; the Atlantic was wide and dangerous in winter. The worst danger was that he might be captured by the British. A former officer of the Crown, he had signed the Declaration of Independence and now was on his way to negotiate an alliance between the revolted provinces and Britain's ancient rival. If captured, he could by British law be charged with high treason and hanged for it. With him were his two grandsons, Temple, seventeen, and Benjamin Franklin Bache, seven, to be educated, Franklin hoped, to carry on his public career as his son could now never do. The armed sloop *Reprisal* carried with it the person whom Jane Mecom loved best on earth, and two nephews who were close to a heart which had lost eight sons by death or madness.

Soon there were dangers closer to home. Washington, unsuccessful against the British in New York, was driven across New Jersey. Jane Mecom had to leave threatened Philadelphia as she had left besieged Boston. On December 8 Franklin wrote her from Nantes: "I arrived here safe after a passage of thirty days, somewhat fatigued and weakened by the voyage, which was a rough one; but I recover my strength fast since my landing, and shall be able I hope in a few days to undertake the journey to Paris of about 250 miles. If the postchaises here were as easy as the English, such a journey would be no difficulty. I hope you continue well and happy. Remember me affectionately to Cousin Jenny and to Mr. and Mrs. Greene." He seems to have supposed she would be back in Rhode Island by the time this reached her. "You can have no conception," he said in a postscript, "of the respect with which I am received and treated here by the first people, in my private character; for as yet I have assumed no public one."

On the fifteenth, long of course before she could receive his letter from France, Jane wrote him from Goshen, in Chester County, Pennsylvania. "I was distressed at your leaving us, but as affairs have turned out I have blessed God you were absent, and we have reason to hope you are safe arrived at your port. On hearing the enemy were advancing towards us we"—the Baches and she—"thought it necessary to retire to this place, where we hope we are safe and are very comfortable. I have another mercy to be thankful for, which has given great ease to my mind, the return of my Son-in-law Collas, who has by the recommendation of Cousin Williams and Captain [Nathaniel] Falconer (who happened to be then in Boston), obtained the command of a Continental ship. Expects to go to France, and is the bearer of this. I hope he will acquit himself properly in his station. I know nothing of his abilities, but that he has always borne a good character. Our family are all well. Will"—the infant Hercules—"as hearty and lovely as ever, says he wants to go to France to Grandpapa and he must send a boat for him. We shall be very happy to hear from you, from Temple and Benny. Remember my love to them. I suppose your son and daughter will write and inform of all necessary."

She can hardly have heard yet about her blackest misfortune of that year. "You I doubt not remember," she wrote her brother two years later, "you had engaged for the support of poor Benjamin in his deplorable state. He never could be kept in the place you expected, but was wandering about till the Hessians took possession of Burlington," which was December 11, "when he disappeared and has never been heard of since." In another letter she said it was "soon after the battle at Trenton," on December 26, that Benny disappeared. If the date is uncertain, so are the mode and place of his death. On the twenty-ninth of that month, he was, or would have been, forty-four. And on that day she could wonder whether he had perhaps stumbled into some ditch beside a muddy road and lain there rotting; or slipped into the Delaware and drifted out to sea in the broken ice; or, the best she could wish for, found someone to show him a little kindness as he wandered bewildered and desperate, or to give him even the roughest burial in some anonymous, unrecorded grave.

7

The Want of Suitable
Conversation

WASHINGTON'S victories at Trenton late in December 1776 and at Princeton early in January put off the British threat to Philadelphia, but only for a time; and after Brandywine Jane Mecom again fled from an occupying army and in September left for Rhode Island. Her granddaughter Jane Flagg was now married to Elihu Greene and lived at Coventry. Elihu sent Major Samuel Ward, nephew and soon to be son-in-law to Catharine Greene, with a phaeton all the way to Philadelphia to escort the refugee to a safer place. She explained to her brother in May 1778 that because her grandson-in-law "had married my granddaughter very poor, and you have generously bestowed on me wherewithal to provide for myself . . . I paid a third of the whole expense, which with a few trifles I brought to use on the road cost me about seventy dollars. The rest of the money I had I have put to interest, which is about four hundred dollars"—the capital, not the interest—"and is what I have to depend on. I am at no expense at present, enjoying health, peace, and competence in my grandson's family, who is a very good sort of man of plain sense and sound judgment, whose conversation is agreeable when he talks, but that is but little. My child makes him

134

a frugal, industrious, and discreet wife, and they are very happy. She had a fine child, but has lost it. I am determined to make what I have answer my purpose by wearing my old clothes over again and purchasing nothing but what is absolutely necessary, such as shoes which one can't do without, but are now at such a price in this place that I have purchased seven pair in Boston when I lived there for what one pair costs here of the same sort."

Elihu Greene and his brothers had a house and a forge at Coventry and a house, a grist mill, and another forge at Potowomut near the William Greenes' house at Warwick. At one house or the other, with frequent visits to Catharine Greene's, Jane spent most of the next four years. She could not escape from the British, it appeared, for they had taken Newport before she arrived, and they held it till October 1779. There were raids on the shores of Narragansett Bay, once within a mile of Potowomut, and after William Greene was elected governor of the state in May 1778 the British put a price on his head. But Jane Mecom was troubled less because the enemy was so near than because her brother was so far away, and so difficult to hear from. Once for a period of three years not a single letter of his reached her, though hers to him had better luck.

One of hers, written in February 1779, closed the long account of her distracted sons. "My dear dear Brother," she said, "myself and children have always been a heavy tax upon you, but your great and uncommon goodness has carried you cheerfully on under it, and we have all along enjoyed many of the comforts of life, through your bounty, we must otherwise have done without. It has pleased God to diminish us fast and thereby your expense and care of us." Here she spoke of the disappearance of her son Benjamin after the battle at

Trenton. "This I informed you of soon after, but your never mentioning it to me in either of the few letters I received from you, I think it did not reach you. It has now pleased God to take poor Peter, and by that has relieved me from great distress, for though I still retained for him the affection of a parent, the great difficulties of the times, and the extreme demands of the woman where he boarded continually increasing"—up to five depreciated dollars a week—"and my inability to satisfy them, and not being able to procure him any other place of residence by any means, kept me in perpetual anxiety. And you know he has been no comfort to any one nor capable of enjoying himself for many years. His mouth was opened just before his death, to commit himself to the mercy of God and wish a blessing on those about him; and sunk into eternity without a groan. Mr. Williams has kindly and faithfully taken the care of everything concerning him in my absence. I now thank you and him. What could I have done without either of you? You have supplied the means, he has taken the care. May God reward you and make you happy in your own posterity!"

There was little comfort to be had from Jane Collas, the last survivor of Jane Mecom's twelve children. Jenny Collas seemed to her mother, she wrote to Sarah Bache, "a poor low-spirited creature when anything befalls her." Early in 1778 Jenny came to visit her mother at Coventry, and in April and May of that year Jane Mecom wrote her daughter two letters that display the characters of the two women as nothing else in the record does.

"That I always did love you," the first of the letters began, "I think I have all along in life given manifest proof, though my circumstances did not admit shewing it in the manner you wished; and that I do still love you my own heart as well as my late conduct is a sufficient witness to myself." Her late conduct had included some reproof of Jenny's idleness and pretensions, and Jenny had promised full reformation. "I am far from desiring you to perform all you profess to be willing to do, but some alteration in the disposition I observed in you when here, there must be or I should not be happy. I see your fondness for a great deal of company is not at all abated, and that is exceeding disagreeable to me. Your aspiring so much to gentility, without means to support it, must appear as ridiculous in every prudent person's eye as it does in mine, though it does not concern them to let you know it; and your lying abed in a morning was always a trouble to me on many accounts, your health one of the principal. You wrote me from Wells you had tried the experiment of rising early and found your health much improved; but I found by your own relation of Mrs. Gray's maid's coming in and making your breakfast before you were up, you have relapsed into the same practice. It has often so fretted me to wait for you to come to breakfast that I could not get over it in some hours.

"Those are some of the reasons why I appeared indifferent about going to live with you, from which little vexatious incidents would so often accrue that it would keep my mind perpetually uneasy. My natural temper is none of the patientest, and though by age and experience I am brought in some measure to check the appearance of resentment, I don't know but I am as much inwardly galled as ever, therefore think it prudent to avoid such occasions as much as may be. But, after all, whenever I hear you are settled in any place that you can entertain me, you may depend on my coming to make a trial, still retaining the resolution which I suppose gave you offense . . . that I must spend the remainder of my life where I can enjoy most ease and happiness. It is natural to wish for ease and quiet at my years." She was sixty-six.

Jane Collas had said in a letter that she thought Jane Greene ought to put her brother Josiah Flagg, crippled in childhood and now living with an uncle in Lancaster, Massachusetts, "in a way to get a genteel living." Jane Mecom pointed out that this was impossible. Jane Greene had no money of her own, and her husband was "obliged to do the meanest drudgery himself, by reason help is not to be had, and their frequent losses will put it still further out of his power. . . . They have this morning received intelligence of two more of their vessels' being taken. . . . William says this is nine vessels taken during the war in which they had property, and that it will make them little folks. That was his expression."

And there was the matter of Jane Greene's reception of Jane Collas, when she arrived at Coventry. That had appeared "reproachable, and I did not fail to speak my mind," Jane Mecom wrote. But Jane Greene had on that occasion been in distress over her husband's losses, and near the birth of her first child, and had come "into the room with her eyes full of tears and her heart ready to burst. . . . Her fears and distress at that time, we have reason to think, has been one means of the death of her child"—Celia—"who from its birth started at every the least noise till it was taken with convulsion fits which ended its days at two months old" in March.

In May Jane Mecom replied to a long letter she had had from Jane Collas. "You say," the mother wrote, "you will endeavor to correct all your faults. It is not among the least that you suffer yourself to look always on the dark side of God's

Providence towards you. Recollect the extent of that expression, 'you have experienced every distress this miserable world could inflict on you,' and you will find yourself mistaken; but were it so, the world has it not in his power to affect us so much as we may receive by God's immediate hand. I never informed you of half I met with, but you know enough to see a vast disproportion between what I have had to undergo and what you have met with. If the loss of near and dear relations is an affliction, I have buried the best of parents, all my sisters and brethren except one, how many of my children and in what circumstances you know, and some small remembrance of my difficulties before your father's death and after you must have: which, if I had done as you do, might have sunk me into despair. But I have always tried to recollect the mercies afforded me and the blessings I still enjoy, and endeavor to be thankful, which is the method you must take if you mean to make the best improvement of your sufferings. For it cannot be acceptable to the Divine Being to have us always repining and take no notice of His mercies when we receive so many more than we deserve. Let us submit to His will and be cheerful.

"This you may assure yourself, if it is any comfort to you, that in all your afflictions I am afflicted, and, were it in my power, would alleviate them all; and had I a sufficient income to support us together, you should not be liable to the impositions of such complaisant folks as make extravagant demands while they pretend to oblige you (but I hope it will not be long before your husband comes home, and then all will be well again).

"I have never yet seen it possible for us to live together, unless we could be willing to spend all we had in a year and have nothing to depend on, as we should not have stock sufficient to go into any business that would support us these times, and what little I have would soon run out were I to pay for my board; therefore we must look on all as an over-ruling Providence which may turn out for the best at last. . . . I am apt to think you might have been as happy in some plain country farmer's house, and at much less expense than where you are"—boarding with William Gooch, one of the Boston cousins, and his wife Deborah Hubbart, another of them. "Then it might not have been thought improper for you to have done some work, both for profit and amusement"—as both Catharine Greene and Jane Mecom had recently done at Warwick. Jane Collas, if she had seen it, might have "had the example of the Governor's lady and the Ambassador's sister making ruffled shirts and stockings for the soldiers, who were in great want and could not get hands enough to supply them. All the families in this place assisted and were paid for it, as they knew not who they should give it to if they did not.

"Another thing, I believe, I recommended to you once before, which was to exchange works with the country people. You might get yourself spinning and weaving done, and at the same time keep yourself constantly employed, which could contribute greatly to a composed mind. I find I cannot live without it. Mrs. Bache got a great deal done so, and so has Jenny [Greene] since I put her in the way of it; and you can not only do plain work, but make bonnets, cloaks, caps, and anything. You ought to see that it is only in your imagination that I am more severe to your mistakes than to others. You know it was always my judgment and practice, if I had occasion to reprove any one, to do it to themselves"—not talk behind their backs. "Perhaps I am too severe with every one, and I am told with myself too."

II

Jane Collas did not notably change her ways. She had early come to the conclusion that there was no family so unfortunate as the Mecoms, and she found that her husband was as unlucky as any Mecom. His persistent misfortunes, which began about the time Benjamin Mecom died, ran through the rest of Jane Mecom's life as if her son-in-law were expected to follow the precedent of her sons.

Captain Peter Collas is said to have been a native of Guernsey. The earliest mention of him found in Boston appears to be his marriage to the younger Jane Mecom in March 1773. When hostilities broke out he was at sea, on a vessel out of Salem, and the natural cause of great anxiety to his wife, then boarding in Roxbury. Her reason for this was the same as that she gave in a later letter to her "dear and ever honored Uncle" in Paris: "At present I am obliged to leave all my friends and retire to country lodging to save expenses. A person must have a good income to be able to live in town, everything is so very dear."

To avoid the British blockade of Salem, Collas put in at New Bedford soon after Lexington and Concord. There was an interval unaccounted for in the record, and then the next year he was given, on the recommendation of Jonathan Williams, Sr., and Franklin's old friend Captain Nathaniel Falconer, command of an unidentified "Continental ship" and set out for France. Collas was captured early in the voyage by the British, held for some months on a prison ship at New York, and exchanged in June 1777. He believed, Jane Mecom wrote her brother, "that the mention of his wife's being a relation of yours was the means of her getting her petition answered in sending a person to exchange for him." In September of that year Collas went as first lieutenant on the brigantine *Starks,* Captain John Allen Hallet. Within a year he had been taken again and then again, as Jane Mecom said in a letter to her brother in August 1778. "He has had nothing but misfortune and sickness," she wrote; since his imprisonment in New York "twice taken, once drove back in port by storm to refit." She now supposed he had been taken a third time; and he had. On this voyage he sailed from Boston on the *Triton* in January, and by March was captured and, after eight days on his native Guernsey, put in prison in England, at Plymouth. He insisted he had taken every precaution to avoid every vessel, but had put too much faith in a pilot who told him that a British ship they sighted was an American privateer. Through Franklin's efforts Collas was released, visited France, saw Franklin and John Adams at Passy, sailed from Nantes that summer, and was once more taken by a Guernsey frigate. Released yet again, he wrote from Nantes in January 1779 to thank Franklin for his many favors. Collas would, he said, follow Franklin's advice and, back in Boston, try to learn how to make crown soap. Franklin evidently thought that Collas did not belong at sea in wartime.

Jonathan Williams, Sr., who had known Collas for several years, wrote to Franklin in July in reply to a letter Collas had brought to Boston. The business of making crown soap which Franklin proposed, Williams said, "partly for the benefit of your worthy sister," he could not approve of if Collas was to be concerned in it. "I shall always be happy to advance any moneys for the benefit of my much esteemed Aunt. . . . However, this I have found, when I have advanced moneys for persons who depended on me for their support and put them into business, it cost me more than maintaining of them entirely; though I believe Aunt would have had something beforehand [ahead] if all that were a burden to her were out of the way. For as long as some people can find dependence they will not provide for themselves, though they might do it if they would be as industrious as those that maintain them." There were then no persons dependent on Jane Mecom but the Collases. Cousin Williams evidently thought that Collas would not succeed in business anywhere at any time.

Collas and his wife went to Rhode Island to visit Jane Mecom that summer. Catharine Greene wrote her great friend in Passy that Collas had given them "an agreeable history of Doctor Franklin, which is pleasing to us as we love to hear of your health and your releasing us from the British yoke." Jane Mecom informed her brother that as Collas could not see his way to settling on shore she could not believe there was any prospect of making enough crown soap to support a family.

After so many nautical mishaps, Collas found it difficult to get another ship, and had to "hitch along in the world," his mother-in-law wrote in December 1780, as well as he could on small trading vessels along the coast. His wife "boards in the country commonly while he is at sea; he makes a shift to pay for that when he comes home; they are now at housekeeping at Cambridge, as he could not git a house in Boston to suit them." There was a third Jane Mecom with them: a daughter of Benny Mecom. He and his wife had tried to persuade Jane Collas at the time of her marriage to take the child, then about eight years old. "But," the grandmother wrote, "we have been obliged to leave her to the care of strangers."

When the Collases first set up housekeeping at Cambridge, the eldest Jane Mecom later wrote, Collas was supposed, presumably on his own statements, to have "got much by privateering"; but a short time after his mother-in-law came to live with them in 1782, she found "he had hired money on interest to live on, which was then near expended. I all the while let them have money for necessaries, and it was accounted as pay for my board, but there was no prospect of better doings, he going daily to Boston to seek for business and finding none. I asked him why he did not get a house and remove there. He said he could not"—she supposed for want of credit. His rent in Cambridge, she discovered, was two years unpaid. It was this which decided her, about the end of 1783, to go with the Collases to the house in Unity Street which had once been her sister Elizabeth Douse's and had long been rented for the support of her son Peter. Jane had to lend Collas money to settle with his Cambridge landlord and leave for Boston.

Jane Collas, in a later letter to her uncle, declared that her husband was "a very industrious, active man, a sweet, kind, benevolent disposition, has ever been very tender of me and does all he can for me; his errors are of the head and not of the heart." Jane Collas's heart was no judge of a head. Her husband was incompetent and untrustworthy, an annoyance and a burden to her mother through all the years of her exile from Boston, and later.

III

During those years of exile the correspondence between Jane Mecom and her brother, however interrupted, was the source of her fullest life and her freest expression. A report, emanating from England, that an attempt to assassinate Franklin had left him "in a languishing condition" in Paris, came to America early in 1778 and made, Jane wrote him in May, "many a heart to tremble." But on the same ship with the report came a letter from her brother to Catharine Greene, telling her about the successful conclusion of the treaty with

France. "I pity my poor old sister," he said, "to be so harassed and driven about by the enemy; for I feel a little myself the inconvenience of being driven about by my friends." Jane, replying to this and an earlier letter, now lost, to her, could thank God both for her brother's safety and for the treaty under which "we may be restored to peace on our own equitable terms of established independence."

In August she wrote him that, now the Elihu Greenes had moved from inland Coventry to the more exposed Potowomut, she had been, with them, "in constant jeopardy since the spring." Elihu and two of his brothers, besides the General, were in the forces engaged in expelling the British from Newport. "You will acknowledge this is rather worse than being harried about by one's friends, yet I doubt not but that is troublesome to you who are so desirous of retirement. I fear you will never be suffered to enjoy it." She repeated some of the things she had told him about her mad sons in a letter which she supposed had been lost. "I write this with great reluctance, but as you desired me to inform you of my circumstances, as well as health and situation, it will not be confiding in you as such a friend as you have always been to me, and perhaps the only disinterested one I have in the world, to keep it back."

In February 1779, after telling him about the death of her son Peter, she said she could hear nothing from her daughter, who was so "apt to sink under trouble. . . . May God preserve her from the fate of her brothers. Pardon my writing you these apprehensions. I do not take pleasure in giving you an uneasy thought, but it gives me some relief to unbosom one's self to a dear friend as you have been and are to me: father, husband, brother, and children. May I not live to be deprived of all in you!"

Franklin, replying in April before he had heard of Peter Mecom's death, told her she mentioned letters he had never received from her. "Don't, however, be discouraged from writing as often as you can; for I am uneasy when long without hearing from you; and the chance is greater that one letter out of many should arrive than one out of a few. . . . If you do not hear from me so often as formerly, impute it to the too much business upon my hands and the miscarriage of letters, or anything rather than the diminution of affection. . . .

"I continue to enjoy, thanks to God, a greater share of health and strength than falls to the lot of many of my age. I have indeed sometimes moderate fits of the gout; but I think it is not settled among the physicians whether that is a disease or a remedy. I live about two miles out of the City [Paris], in a great garden that has pleasant walks in which I can take exercise in a good air, the situation being high and dry. The village [Passy] has many good houses and good families with whom I live in friendship and pass a leisure hour, when I have one, with pleasure. The French in general are an amiable people, and I have the good fortune to enjoy as much of the esteem of all ranks as I have any pretensions to. Temple continues with me; but I have last week sent Benny [Bache] to Geneva, where there are as good schools as here, and where he will be educated a republican and a Protestant, which could not be so conveniently done at the schools in France."

In June Jane wrote a letter teasing her brother about an anecdote which had been invented in England and reprinted in various American newspapers. "A gentleman just returned from France," the *London Chronicle* said, "informs us that Dr. Franklin has shaken off entirely the mechanical rust, and commenced the complete courtier. Being lately in the gardens of Versailles, showing the Queen some electrical experiments, she asked him, in a fit of raillery, if he did not dread the fate of Prometheus, who was so severely served for stealing fire from heaven? 'Yes, please your Majesty,' replied old Franklin with infinite gallantry, 'if I did not behold a pair of eyes this moment which have stolen infinitely more fire from Jove than ever I did, pass unpunished, though they do more mischief in a week than I have done in all my experiments.' " Referring to this nonsense, Jane Mecom wrote: "Bless God I now and then hear of your health and glorious achievements in the political way, as well as in the favor of the ladies ('since you have rubbed off the mechanic rust and commenced complete courtier'), who Jonathan Williams [Jr.] writes me claim from you the tribute of an embrace, and it seems you do not complain of the tax as a very great penance. . . .

"I see few persons of your acquaintance, which deprives me of much pleasure I used to have in conversing about you; but now and then I see something in the paper which pleases me: in particular, their placing you in one of the arches at the exhibition made on the anniversary of the French treaty." The exhibition had been held at Washington's artillery park at Pluckemin, New Jersey, on February 18, and newspapers throughout the country reported it. The fireworks that evening displayed thirteen arches, in each of which was an "illuminated painting," on transparent cloth. As the lights flared up behind the arches, the audience saw a symbolic panorama of the war and its significance. Only two of the arches were devoted to a single hero each. The sixth was "a grand illuminated representation of Louis the Sixteenth, the encourager of letters, the supporter of the rights of humanity, the ally and friend of the American republic." The eighth arch

showed "The American philosopher and ambassador"—no
need to name him in this company—"extracting lightning
from the clouds." Jane Mecom's brother.

In July she replied to a lost letter of the past November
with which he had sent her a substantial gift of goods or
money. "You, like yourself," she said, "do all for me that the
most affectionate brother can be desired or expected to do.
And though I feel myself full of gratitude for your generosity,
the conclusion of your letter affects me more: where you say
you wish we may spend our last days together. O my brother,
if this could be accomplished it would give me more joy than
anything on this side heaven could possibly do. I feel the
want of suitable conversation," such as she had had with him
in those golden months in Philadelphia. "I have but little here.
I think I could assume more freedom with you now, and com-
vince you of my affection for you; for I have had time to
reflect and see my error in that respect. I suffered my diffidence and the awe of your superiority to prevent the famili-
arity I might have taken with you, and ought, and your
kindness to me might have convinced me would be acceptable. But it is hard overcoming a natural propensity, and diffidence is mine."

These words marked a kind of turning-point in her relations with Franklin. Heretofore it had been hard for her to
write her heart to him, though under stress she had often done
so. Hereafter she did it with lessening self-consciousness.

"It is a very happy circumstance that you enjoy your health
so perfectly. It is a blessing vouchsafed to me also, except
some trifling interruption, and that but seldom: which I a
good deal attribute to my observation of your former admoni-
tions respecting fresh air and diet. For whatever you may
think, every hint of yours appeared of too much consequence

to me to be neglected or forgotten; as I always knew everything you said had a meaning.

"The few friends I have here flock about me when I receive a letter, and are much disappointed that they contain no politics. I tell them you dare not trust a woman [with] politics, and perhaps that is the truth. But if there is anything we could not possibly misconstrue or do mischief by knowing from you, it will gratify us mightily if you add a little to your future kind letters."

Franklin could not now confide in her, as he had done in England. His letters from France were always subject to seizure by alert British cruisers, and his diplomatic moves had to be reported to Congress with the utmost discretion.

He had asked her to send him some of the best crown soap for presents to his friends, but she was afraid she could not do it, she wrote, "till the new wax comes in; for I have tried shops and acquaintance here, and cannot procure any. The country people put it into their summer candles. I have desired Cousin Jonathan to try to pick up a little in the shops there [in Boston], and shall try at Providence. I am sorry to be deprived of the pleasure of gratifying you, but my power was always small, though my will is good." And she ended with a prayer that brother and sister might some day live together.

By September she had made two dozen cakes of the soap, at Governor Greene's house, "but not of the very best possible, as you desired, owing to some unavoidable impediments, but sent it notwithstanding, as it will answer for your own use, and Temple's, but would wish you not to make any presents of it." She was distressed to hear of his fits of the gout, but happy that he lived among agreeable companions. "The respect and admiration of all sensible people wherever you go, I am sure you can not fail of, but it is a great satisfaction to have a number of them so near you that you may take your own time to go to them. I have not the privilege of one neighbor nearer than two miles, but we have many agreeable people come to visit us, and I am always contented at home, and pleased to go abroad when sent for. Otherways I cannot go, for our people have no carriage and I han't courage to ride a horse. . . .

"When"—and she here returned to a thought that now seldom left her—"shall I have any foundation for the hope that we shall again meet and spend our last days together? America knows your consequence too well to permit your return if they can possibly prevent it; and your care for the public good will not suffer you to desert them till peace is established. And the dismal sound of 'fifteen years from the commencement of the war' dwells on my mind, which I once heard you say it might last. If it does, it is not likely I shall last that long, but that you may continue in health and usefulness is the constant prayer of your affectionate sister."

Franklin's letter of October was partly in reply to hers of February about the death of Peter Mecom. Her brother said as little as possible about her grief, so as to avoid stirring it up again after the enforced delay. But what he said had in it all his art and all his knowledge of what would best comfort her. The news had brought him, he said, "a kind of melancholy satisfaction. The greater ease you will now enjoy makes some compensation in my mind for the uncomfortable circumstance that brought it about. I hope you will have no more afflictions of that kind, and that after so long and stormy a day your evening may be serene and pleasant."

Then, as usual, he turned lightly to a lighter topic she had brought up. "The account you had from Jonathan Williams of the vogue I am in here, has some truth in it. Perhaps few strangers in France have had the good fortune to be so universally popular. But the story you allude to which was in the newspapers, mentioning 'mechanic rust,' etc. is totally without foundation. The English papers frequently take those liberties with me. I remember to have once counted seven paragraphs relating to me that came by one post, all of which were lies except one that only mentioned my living in the same house with Mr. [Silas] Deane. This popularity has occasioned so many paintings, bustos, medals, and prints to be made of me, and distributed throughout the kingdom, that my face is now almost as well known as that of the moon. But one is not to expect being always in fashion. I hope, however, to preserve, while I stay here, the regard you mention of the French ladies, for their society and conversation, when I have time to enjoy it, is extremely agreeable."

Because in July his sister had asked for some little item of political news that she and her friends might safely know, he told her a few dependable facts about the recent attacks by Commodore John Paul Jones on British shipping. "Had not contrary winds and accidents prevented it, the intended invasion of England with the combined fleet and a great army might have taken place, and have made the English feel a little more of that kind of distress they have so wantonly caused in America."

Late in September that year Ezra Stiles, president of Yale, dined one day at Governor Greene's house, and talked with Jane Mecom about her brother. Stiles, who had delivered a Latin oration on Franklin at Yale in 1755, and who ten years later was made a doctor of divinity by the University of Edinburgh on Franklin's recommendation, knew the philosopher only as a famous man. Now he could learn something about the great man's youth, and here was the one person alive who knew most about it and was happiest to tell the story. She showed Stiles the famous epitaph which Franklin had written on himself as printer, and let Stiles copy it from her copy, which was in Franklin's hand, and which she thought had been originally composed "twenty years ago"—though it was almost certainly older. Franklin had probably given her the copy in Philadelphia when she was with him there. Jane told Stiles about the coming of her father from Ecton, Northamptonshire, to New England, and his second marriage to Abiah Folger. Jane's talk ran on, and Stiles later made notes of what she told him, more or less in the order of her telling.

"Dr. Franklin was the youngest son, and Jane Mecom the youngest daughter (I think) who was born March 27, 1712. He [Josiah Franklin] belonged to Rev. Dr. Sewall's church and died December 1, 1744 *aet.* 89." This date was wrong (like the age), but may have been Stiles' mistake for what he heard. "His wife died 1752 *aet.* 85. The Doctor read his Bible at five years old." At seven he wrote some verses, "a specimen of his ingenuity," which were sent to his Uncle Benjamin in England and brought back the comment, also in verse: "If the buds are so precious, what may we expect when the fruit is ripe." What Uncle Benjamin wrote was actually: "For, if the bud bear grain, what will the top?" Jane had forgotten the exact words, which reached Boston when she was only one. Franklin "learned Latin chiefly himself, though he went to the Latin School in Boston. Studied incessantly a-nights when a boy. Addicted to all kinds of reading. His brother James was a printer in Boston, with whom he lived an apprentice; and after some political quarrels the *Courant* was printed in Benjamin's name. Upon his Brother James's removing his press to Newport, Benjamin went to

Philadephia at seventeen." Perhaps Jane had forgotten the actual date of James' removal, or perhaps she preferred merely not to tell that Benjamin had been a runaway apprentice. "Afterwards he went to London and worked journey work about two years, and then returned and set up his business in Philadelphia. His Uncle Benjamin came over also and settled in Dr. Colman's church in Boston, where he died a good old man. Dr. Colman preached his funeral sermon on 'Mark the perfect man.'"

All this, Stiles recorded, he had "*ex ore* the Doctor's sister." And then he added: "Governor Franklin now *aet.* forty-seven, *ex ore* Mrs. Mecom his aunt." The age here given for William Franklin made him appear to be at least a year younger than he was, and consequently to have been born a respectable time after Franklin's marriage to Deborah Read. Jane may have been honestly in error, or she may have preferred to keep to herself the family secret about William's birth.

"The agreeable situation of your dwelling," she wrote to her brother in March 1780, "beautiful gardens, and your choice of the best of company I often form to myself an idea of; and wish you could enjoy them here with the same benefit to your native country. You are happy in that you can never want friends, go where you will; and as far as it is possible for any created being, will remain in fashion. But if the artists that have taken your face have varied as much from each other as that affixed to your Philosophical Papers [*Œuvres de M. Franklin*] done in France some years ago [1773] from the [English] copy, it will appear as changeable as the moon. However, if it is called Dr. Franklin it will be revered. In my last letter I wrote to beg a couple of those prints, or bustos, either which is thought most like you and that can be easiest or safest conveyed. I seldom meet with anything in the newspapers but what is to your honor. That of the 'mechanic rust' served only to make me laugh. . . .

"I have sent in the French frigate that Mr. [John] Adams went in a small box of soap containing but two dozen. I thought I could have made a little more better, but I don't think I have succeeded."

As the months of this year and the next went by with no letter from Franklin, Jane Mecom herself wrote less frequently. But when Ralph Izard, who had been jealous and envious of Franklin in Paris and suspected him of paying too much attention to the interests of France, arrived in the United States, she felt called upon to report to her brother in December. "As I hear from good authority that you are well and do well, I am the less concerned at the endeavors of some to defame your character, but not perfectly easy about it, for I fear there is too much truth in that common saying 'where much dirt is thrown some will stick,' though I perceive none at present in this case. One Izard was very laborious at Newport to make people believe you had done something criminal in many matters respecting the men belonging to the [American frigate] *Alliance*, pretending he had strong vouchers he was carrying with him to Congress. He was asked what he thought was your motive. He would give no other than that you had a nephew [Jonathan Williams, Jr.] there you wanted to assist in making a fortune. General Greene's wife was in his company when he run on so, and she advised him not to speak disrespectful of you on the road, for the people would have a bad opinion of him. But she heard afterwards by a gentleman that came from camp . . . that he had made it his business at every stage and intended to do so till he got to Congress. I have heard nothing of him since, and it is some months ago. I fancy by the time he got there he sunk into oblivion."

Impossible for Jane Mecom to believe that Izard, and Arthur Lee who was of Izard's opinion, would devote themselves for the rest of Franklin's life and later to implacable animosity toward the man who had been their chief in Paris. Franklin, writing to Richard Bache about Lee and Izard, called them "those unhappy gentlemen: unhappy indeed in their tempers, and in the dark, uncomfortable passions of jealousy, anger, suspicion, envy, and malice. . . . I take no other revenge of such enemies than to let them remain in the miserable situation in which their malignant natures have placed them."

From Ralph Izard, Jane turned to the family of Elihu Greene. "My granddaughter has had two children in seventeen months. The eldest is a daughter, Sally, the other a son, Franklin: not because we could forgit your name but that we love to hear it. We left out the Benjamin that he might not be called Ben." She closed with a postscript: "My love to Temple and Benny [Bache], when you write to him. Do write me something about them or persuade Temple to spend an hour in gratifying his old aunt."

Tenderly as she loved her granddaughter Jane Greene and her children, Jane Mecom found that her life as great-grandmother was harder on her than her life as mother and grandmother had been. "I am still in tolerable health," she wrote her brother in March 1781, "and every way as comfortable excepting that as I grow older I wish for more quiet, and our family is more encumbered. We have had three children since I came; and though they give great pleasure in common, yet the noise of them is sometimes troublesome. I have often heard you wish for liberty to live more retired, but it is what neither of us have much grounds to hope for. I often contemplate the happiness it would afford me to have you settled in a country seat in New England, and I have permission to reside with you, that we might end our days together, retired from all but a few choice ones that would give and receive mutual enjoyment and make us forget any little disagreeable incidents that would unavoidably happen while we remain in the body."

In June: "It is so long since I have had a line from you that if I had not had a former reproof from you"—now lost—"I should be almost ready to conclude on the last of the six chances you then described as reasons for my not receiving letters: that you were tired of corresponding with me and resolved to write no more." Even Jane Mecom, with her miffy temper, could smile at that. She mentioned a satirical poem that the loyalist "Parson [Jonathan] Odell" had written "on your invention of the chamber fireplace. . . . I have half a mind to send it to you, as I think it would make you laugh; but if you should be coming home, it will serve to divert you here. I continue very easy and happy here," now forgetful of the noisy children; "have no more trouble than what is incident to human nature and can't be avoided in any place. I write now in my own little chamber, the window opening on one of the pleasantest prospects in the country, the birds singing about me, and nobody up in the house near me to disturb me."

That fall Jane Mecom went to visit her daughter Jane Collas in Cambridge. The daughter was "in much better health than usual, but her husband after making one successful voyage, is again in the hands of the enemy, in Halifax. . . . I am this day going to Boston in pursuit of a collection of all your works which I hear is lately come from Europe"—

his *Political, Miscellaneous, and Philosophical Pieces* which had been published in London two years before, and received with general praise in spite of his English reputation as the prime mover of the American rebellion. Some of the pieces in this collection she had formerly had, and had lost: "You will say then I don't deserve to have them again, but maybe not if you knew all the circumstances. However, there is many things I never had, and I can hardly help envying any one that pleasure without my partaking."

From Boston later in October she wrote to acknowledge the receipt from him of a "large package . . . of considerable value, but have not yet time to know exactly. They are things much sought for by our dressing ladies which will procure money, though I thank God, and you, I have not wanted any good thing. I live very comfortable with my grandchildren for good living in the family, and your bounty supplies me with all I ought to wish besides your good company." And there was the news of Yorktown printed in the *Boston Gazette* on the day she wrote. "The glorious news we have now received from the southward," she said, "makes us flatter ourselves you may return to us soon: and Mr. Williams says, live and enjoy health and happiness twenty years yet. I have no such expectations for myself, but I wish those a blessing I may leave behind."

Some of the "Silk for cloaks etc., gauze, lace, ribbon, linen, and cambric" which Franklin had sent his sister from France she used for herself or her family, or perhaps in the informal trading she did in Rhode Island. "The rest," she told her brother, "I sold and put the money to interest." Once more with Jane Greene at Potowomut, Jane Mecom entered her last chapter of grief for dead children, almost fifty-two years after her own first-born died.

On Christmas Eve Jane Greene gave birth to her fourth child, yet another Jane. The mother died in April, at twenty-five. In June Jane Mecom wrote to her brother: "Since my return home my time and attention has been filled with sickness and death in the family, in particular that of my dear granddaughter Jenny, who died of a consumption; has left three sweet babes, one about two [four] months old, a sorrowful husband and a distressed grandmother. I enjoyed sweet peace in her pleasant conversation and great comfort in her dutiful and tender attention; was pleased with the hopes of the continuance of it the remainder of my life. But those comforts are vanished, and a care devolved on me that I find myself unequal to, that of the children. The youngest is at nurse, but the other two require some person more lively and patient to watch over them continually. My dear child urged me earnestly not to leave them as long as I live, and though I made her no promise I find the request to be very powerful. Her husband is desirous I should continue with him, and treats me very respectfully, that I have no thoughts of removing at present, but circumstances may alter in time. I can't expect it to be otherways, as he is a young man. But my stay in the world may be much shorter, and life becomes less desirable except I should find a capacity to be more useful, which growing infirmities and low spirits prevent. My friend Greene told me she wrote you soon after my child died, and I don't doubt she was more particular than I can be at present, for my little ones are interrupting me every minute, and it is so hot I am not willing to trust them out of my sight. . . . I began this at the Governor's, but was fetched home to the funeral of my grandson's brother's wife, who died in the same house with us."

Catharine Greene wrote Franklin that his sister was "so

fond of the children that I fear it will be a disadvantage to both. She thinks she can't leave them to visit us scarcely."

Jane Mecom wrote again in June, still depressed by her grief and the long apparent silence of her brother, who was just then overwhelmed, so far as he could be overwhelmed, by the intricate preliminary negotiations for peace with England. "Something constantly passes that keeps alive my sorrow, though I have plenty of all necessaries, and the same beautiful prospect around me, and all the season blooming. I do so much miss her society that it spreads a gloom over all."

When the cold weather came that year Jane gave up the struggle and went to Cambridge to spend the winter with her daughter and her unlucky husband. There, Jane Mecom wrote her brother the day after Christmas, she could be "more retired, and less exposed to doors opening on me which in cold weather increases my cough and is very tedious to me. But on my arrival at Boston I had the melancholy account of a distressing fit of illness you have had, though something better when the messenger came away." This was the bladder stone which suddenly incapacitated Franklin early in September, to trouble him with varying degrees of pain all the rest of his life. Now Jane Mecom lost the sense of her own grief in her concern for her brother. "I am frequently reflecting on the pain you endured and the danger of the frequent returns of the disorder you are liable to," as their brother John had been, and died of it when he was ten years younger than Benjamin was now; "and fearing they may be too hard for you. May God who has hitherto given you so much health prevent it, and restore you to perfect health again. If that may not be, I hope you will be endowed with all the submission necessary on so trying an occasion. . . .

"My son Collas and daughter, who is all the child I have

left, and Jenny Mecom (one of my son Benjamin's children) do all in their power to make me comfortable; and I go sometimes to Boston where I am kindly entertained by Cousin Williams and family and see a few other friends. I have one of my deceased granddaughter's children with me and expect to return with it in the spring, as there I live pleasantly all the warm weather, and can do a number of things for him and the children, except he should git him another wife, which I believe there is no great likelihood of, he is so sensible it is impossible to make up his loss. She was indeed an extraordinary wife."

Elihu Greene never did get him another wife. A generation later one of his nephews knew him at Potowomut as "a cheery, hale old man, still active at the forge, still ready to raise the dam gate, and take his seat by the hopper . . . and ever gentle and patient and kind."

8

To Live at Ease in My Old Age

DURING the winter of 1782–83 Jane Mecom had the first serious illness of her life, of which she spoke in a letter to Richard Bache the following April, two weeks after her seventieth birthday: "I have had such an admonition this winter of the suddenness by which I might be called out of this world, which was succeeded by a severe fit of sickness that has taught me to be continually looking to the decisive hour when I shall have no further concern in this world." Bache's letter, written in December, had been long unanswered, but now his "affectionate and obliged Aunt" was her indestructible self again. She asked with tender curiosity about his wife and children, and hoped Sarah Bache might soon send the "long-promised and long-expected favor" of detailed information about not only the children but also "all our agreeable acquaintance we had when I was there. . . . But may I not hope for something better, now the glorious news of peace is arrived: that I shall see some of you? . . . If such a thing should be, I hope they or any other of my acquaintance would take pains to inquire me out and come to see me. I am grown such a vagrant I can't opine the place I may be in, as I have all [my] own four homes: my daughter Collas's here" in Cambridge, "Mr. Williams's in Boston, Governor Greene's, and my grandson Elihu Greene's in War-

161

wick in Rhode Island State. Each of them would receive pleasure in entertaining any of mine or my brother's friends from Philadelphia."

She wrote with the more confidence because of the change in her fortunes of which she had heard in letters, now missing, from Bache and from Franklin. The details too are missing, but her brother had evidently sent her through Bache, along with an order for twenty-five guineas, the promise of an assured income, of an amount not known, for the rest of her life, as well as the income from the house in Unity Street.

Her letter to Franklin that same April spoke first of her joy at hearing from him, so long silent. "I have at length received a letter from you in your own handwriting, after a total silence of three years, in which time part of an old song would sometimes intrude itself into my mind.

> Does he love and yet forsake me?
> For can he forgit me?
> Will he neglect me?

This was but momentary. At other times I concluded it was reasonable to expect it, and that you might with great propriety, after my teasing you so often, send me the answer that Nehemiah did to Tobiah and Sanballat, who endeavored to obstruct his building the Temple in Jerusalem: 'I am doing a great work, so that I cannot come down; why should the work cease, whilst I leave it and come *down* to you.'

"And a great work indeed you have done, God be praised. I hope now you yourself will think you have done enough for the public, and will now put in execution what you have sometimes wished to be permitted to do: sit down and spend the evening with your friends. I am looking round me at Cambridge for a commodious seat for you, not with any great hopes of your coming here, I confess (but wishes), knowing you are accommodated so much to your mind at Philadelphia, and have your children there. I should however expect a share of your correspondence when you have leisure.

"And believe me, my dear Brother, your writing to me gives me so much pleasure that the great, the very great, present you have sent me is but a secondary joy. I have been very sick this winter at my daughter's, kept my chamber six weeks, but had a sufficiency for my supply of everything that could be a comfort to me before I received any intimation of the great bounty from your hand which your letter had conveyed to me. For I have not been lavish of what I before possessed, knowing sickness and misfortunes might happen, and certainly old age. But I shall now be so rich that I may indulge in some small degree a propensity to help some poor creatures who have not the blessings I enjoy.

"My good fortune came to me all together to comfort me in my weak state; for as I had been so unlucky as not to receive the letter you sent me through your son Bache's hands, though he informs me he forwarded it immediately, his letter with a draft for twenty-five guineas came to my hand just before yours, which I have received, and cannot find expression suitable to acknowledge my gratitude. How am I by my dear Brother enabled to live at ease in my old age (after a life of care, labor, and anxiety) without which I must have been miserable!"

She expected to spend the summer in Rhode Island. If her brother should be coming home this year, and arriving in Boston, she hoped he would visit her and the Greenes on his way to Philadelphia. Jonathan Williams, Sr., had visited Franklin in France the past winter. Jane Mecom wished he and Franklin might come back together, "though on second thought I think it will be too valuable a treasure among our families to venture in one bottom. But I shall depend on that Providence which has hitherto been your preserver, protector, and defender."

After a summer at Warwick and Potowomut, where she found that another of Elihu Greene's children, Jane, had died in April, Jane Mecom returned to Cambridge. There she received a letter from Franklin, written in September, who said he was happy "that the little supplies I sent you have contributed to make your life more comfortable. I shall by this opportunity order some more money into the hands of Cousin Williams, to be disposed of in assisting you as you may have occasion.

"Your project of taking a house for us to spend the remainder of our days in is a pleasing one, but it is a project of the heart rather than of the head. You forget, as I sometimes do, that we are grown old, and that before we can have furnished our house, and put things in order, we shall probably be called away from it to a home more lasting, and I hope more agreeable, than any this world can afford us. . . .

"Cousin Williams went back for Boston from London about the beginning of June, so that probably he is with you before this time. He laid out, by my desire, the money he received for you in goods, which you will receive of him. When you have sold them, perhaps it may be advisable to put the money at interest, that it may produce you a little income"—and, Franklin possibly reflected, might be less accessible to the Collases.

When, that fall or early winter, Jane Mecom learned that Peter Collas owed rent for two years on the house in Cambridge, she got the house in Unity Street "cleared as soon as possible," and moved the family to it, "he by written agreement to give me my board for rent." Collas asked her to sign his bond for the debt in Cambridge. "I told him I would not, but I would lend him a consolidated note I had out of our Treasury, of fourteen pound some shillings, which with twelve dollars he had of me before, he settled the affair, so that we were permitted to come away." This was in "the middle of winter," about the first of January.

The Unity Street house, where Jane as a child had often visited her eldest sister Elizabeth Douse, was in need of repairs and at first skimpily furnished. Jane had, it turned out, lost most of her household goods "when the town was ravaged," and not all of her daughter's could be recovered. But the house faced the sun in Unity Street, and at the back looked toward Christ Church, in Salem Street, which had in its steeple a "royal peal" of eight bells, the clearest and most melodious in Boston.

Built of brick, the house had two ample rooms on each of its two floors, with a cellar, and a garret under the gambrel roof. The front door was at the right of anyone who entered, level with the street without a doorstone or stoop. Inside the door was a narrow hall and a stairway to the upper floor. The front room downstairs was the parlor, the back the kitchen. The front room upstairs was for Jane Mecom, who then or later shared it with her granddaughter Jenny Mecom, Benny's daughter. The Collases had the bedroom at the rear, though Captain Collas was often away on his futile ventures.

Now and then in Jane Mecom's letters to her brother during her first year or two in Unity Street she spoke in particulars of this house as she had never spoken of any other in which she lived. "The house is pleasant for light and air," she told him in August 1784, "having a large opening back and forward (as nobody has builded near it since you saw it), and is very convenient for our small family. . . . It is far from the few relations and acquaintance I have in town, but I remember your sentiments are that walking is a most healthful exercise, and I practice it when I am able many times when I am offered a chaise, but am so weak I make but a poor figure in the street." In October: "I am now prettily settled; have had two rooms new papered and painted, have procured some conveniences for my own chamber . . . that if I should be confined to it I might be comfortable, for I can't say I ever feel perfectly well." In May 1785: "I have put a new pump into the well, had it emptied and cleaned to the bottom, had a new platform and sink and all things it wanted, but I had money enough by me to do it." And in May 1786, proudly: "I have this spring been new planking the yard, made [a] new gate and new cedar doors, and am painting the front of the house to make it look decent, that I may not be ashamed when anybody inquires for Dr. Franklin's sister in the neighborhood."

Captain Collas, soon after he moved to Boston, "by some means or other made out to go a sort of trading trip to Nova Scotia, stayed there a great while, and came back with little." Jane Collas, before or after he left, "was taken sick and kept her chamber and almost her bed for three months; was very weak and poorly a long time after and is far from being well now," her mother wrote in August 1784. The main comfort she had was her granddaughter Jenny, now about nineteen, a strong, pleasant girl who had so little of the Mecom frailty that she lived, in time, to be almost a hundred. The strangers who brought her up gave her almost no schooling. At fifteen, her grandmother wrote Sarah Bache, Jenny thought "she should soon write well enough to write to me and her mother." But she was taught "good housewifery," was "hearty and well contented," and after years with strangers was happy to have so kind a grandmother to live with.

The grandmother was so busy with the new house that she did not write to her brother till the July after she moved there. Moreover, she was, she told him, "often affected with great dizziness, and expect or fear if I live much longer to be in such circumstances as Dean Swift was"—that is, insane. "If it pleases God to hear my prayer, death will be much preferable." But she was troubled less by this apprehension than by her grief over her brother's "grievous malady. . . . How many hours have I laid awake on nights, thinking what excruciating pains you might then be encountering. . . . Oh that it was in my power to mitigate or alleviate the anguish I know you must endure!" Now she began to lose hope that she would ever see him again.

In August she received a June letter which told her he was glad to hear she was settled in the house in Boston, "which you may consider as your own, and I hope you will be happy in it. I continue, thanks to God, in very good health, being at present only troubled with the stone; which sometimes gives me a little pain, and prevents my going in a carriage where there are pavements, but does not otherwise make me very unhappy; as I can take the exercise of walking, eat, drink, sleep, read, and write, and enjoy the conversation of my friends as usual."

Replying at once, Jane was afraid he was worse than he admitted. "I know your admirable patience dictates your pen and makes you use the softest terms your case will admit of. Oh I know too much of the anguish you suffer not to feel a constant anxiety for you and think your case hard—very hard. Oh that there was any hope of relief but from cutting [operating to remove the stone], which I suppose at your age you have no thoughts of submitting to! May God continue your patience and not permit the pains to increase!"

She had neglected, she said, to tell him of her "situation and affairs. . . . You are the only person in the world I wish to know all my transactions and the motives to them, as such a friend as my dear Brother would subject me to the least inconveniency. But you long ago convinced me that there is many things proper to converse with a friend about that it is not proper to write." She had, however, to tell him that she no longer felt in herself any "capacity for trading" in the "trunk of gauzes" that Jonathan Williams, Sr., brought her from London; "and if I had, those goods were such a glut they would not fetch the sterling cost, and I did not think myself obliged to take them as he had no reference to me when he purchased them," since they were merely out of the stock he was bringing on his own account. So she accepted Williams' proposal to let her have the value in money, which remained in his hands as part of her capital and would bear interest.

In October 1784 Lafayette, again in America, came to visit his friends in Boston. Jane sent her brother a letter by the "Marquis La Fayette," who she said was "much honored and caressed among us," though there is nothing to indicate that she met him. Again she spoke of her own health. "The similarity of my disorder with Dean Swift's makes me often very apprehensive. I however recreate myself in the best manner I can. I walk abroad often, visit my friends oftener than they do me, hoping they will pay the debt in time of need. I read as much as I dare, but I find it sometimes affects my head. I enjoy all the agreeable conversation I can come at properly, but I find little, very little, equal to what I have a right to by nature but am deprived of by Providence: which however does all things well, and I submit as old Jacob when he found that he had been deprived of the comfort and company of his beloved Joseph for so long a time, since it was of such purposes as to save much people alive."

A part of the town of Wrentham in Massachusetts had in 1778 been set off and incorporated, and named Franklin after the most famous man ever born in Boston. The town asked Franklin in Paris to give them a bell for its church. He gave them books instead, and wrote to Jonathan Williams that the books would be sent from England in his care. "I observe," Jane Mecom wrote her brother in the letter carried by Lafayette, "in one of your letters to Cousin Williams your intention to present to Franklin Town a number of books as a foundation for a parish library, hoping the Franklins will prefer sense to sound. I can't doubt but such a library will consist of some authors on divine subjects. I therefore hope you will not think it too presuming in me to propose one: viz, *Discourses on Personal Religion* in two volumes by Samuel Stennett D.D. printed in London by R. Hett in 1769. I borrowed them and read them with a great deal of pleasure, and I think you yourself would, if you could find time; though there may be many things in them not altogether agreeable to your sentiments—which I suppose may be the case with every volume you read on any subject."

Franklin, asking his friend Richard Price in England to select "a list of a few good books, to the value of about twenty-five pounds" for the library, ventured himself to suggest, besides Price's own books, only this of Stennett's "on the recommendation of my sister." And Jane Mecom, who had borrowed the book from her neighbor Samuel Stillman, minister of the First Baptist Church in Boston, had the pleasure of learning that her recommendation was accepted by her brother and by the learned and famous Richard Price; and that the "Franklins" owed the choice of one book in their library to her.

In May 1785 Jane wrote her brother the last letter she is known to have sent to him in France, in reply to a missing letter from him written in October. It had given her great pleasure, she said, "as it gave me to understand your malady does not increase upon you, but you always represent your afflictions as light as possible to your sister because you know she constantly grieves for you, but I think I can discover you to be in pain even while you thus write. Your tenderness for me in that respect, as in all other virtues, far exceeds mine. For to my regret I reflect that my last letter to you contained too many complaints of my ill state of health and natural decays, which I suppose you had not received. But God has been better to me than my fears, for though it has indeed been a severe winter I have had less indisposition than in either of the two preceding winters. I am however daily looking forward to that state which you once gave me a hint was more proper for my contemplation than seeking a new place of abode in this world.

"However, as it need not impede our journey to that better country, I am strongly inclined to justify my project; as you have professed an inclination to spend your last days in your native place, and I thought you had been so long used to grandeur in your apartments and furniture you had by this time got a surfeit of them and would relish a plain simple accommodation of just conveniences, which would take but little time to supply yourself with, and you had I hoped a number of years before you. Please God you live to the age of your ancestors! But this scheme was before I heard of your distressing calamity. Now alas I fear every year and every day is a burthen to you except you receive some amusement by the wonderful philosophical discoveries lately made in France.

"I have sometimes feared as your old friends in America died off so fast you would be so attached to that country as not to wish to return if your case would permit.

"You have heaped so many blessings upon me I am at a loss how to express my gratitude. I have a great deal of time to contemplate my happy state in abundance of particulars, and thought myself richly provided for in all things necessary for my comfort. The permission you now send me to draw on you for fifty pounds sterling greatly increases the store. I accept with a grateful heart, for I know you give it with pleasure."

And then Jane Mecom closed with a run of gossip and little news. "Would you think it, Captain Partridge that married Betsey Hubbart is gone to be overseer of the Almshouse? I have been to see them since they got there. She appears cheerful and I believe is tolerable contented. Tommy Hubbart," whose first wife had been Judith Ray, Catharine Greene's sister, "is married to a rich widow in the country"—Ann Bigelow, of Weston—"who he was a long time struggling to obtain and has conquered at last. . . .

"My Son Collas is now gone to the eastward to bring a new vessel he is going to the West Indies in. She"—Jane Collas—"is a poor, weakly woman, hardly ever well. Jenny Mecom is still with us, strong and hearty, so there is one in the family free from complaints."

II

During the years when Franklin was in Europe his sister was frequently asked for letters of introduction to him. Knowing how busy he was, she gave such letters with discretion, and as a rule only to persons whom she knew well or who were strongly commended to her. One of these was Patience Wright, who had made a reputation by her portrait models in wax in Philadelphia, increased her reputation in London and Paris, and was a good and useful friend to Franklin. Another was Elkanah Watson, whose later *Men and Times of the Revolution* has engaging records of Franklin's private life at Passy. A third was John Thayer, who cost Jane Mecom and her daughter much contrition and many apologies.

Thayer, born in Boston, educated at Yale, was licensed but not ordained as a Presbyterian (Congregational) minister, and in 1780–81 served as chaplain at Castle William in Boston Harbor. Having made up his mind to go to France, he asked Jane Collas, then living in Cambridge, for a letter of introduction to her uncle. As she later told Franklin the story, Thayer "teased me for months. . . . I all along refused, and begged to be excused from writing at all, telling him I had never presumed to trouble you with my scrawls; but he would not let me rest till he forced from me a few lines of introduction. I gave it him unsealed. In about a week he returned with it and begged I would make some alteration, asked for pen and paper to write the ideas he would wish me to convey. I could not help laughing in his face, though I complied with his request. Mamma was then with me at Cambridge, and after I had perused what he had wrote for me to copy, I told him I could not possibly write a line more than I had wrote, but as I had no reason to doubt the truth of what he had written, I would oblige him by signing my name, and beg the favor of Mamma to do the same; which would put an end, I hoped, to all further trouble. Mamma laughed very heartily at the drollery, and the poor fellow, with all his assurance, looked greatly mortified. I pitied and spared him to plead his cause with Mamma, which he did so effectively as to get a letter of recommendation from her, though she never saw him before. But I never wrote any other than the first I gave him, which could not be called a recommendation, and if you received such a one from me he must have wrote it himself."

Jane Collas's letter, dated June 6, 1781, was no more a letter of recommendation than she said. "The bearer of this is Mr. Thayer, a young gentleman educated at New Haven College, has been some time a candidate for the ministry and chaplain at the Castle, is now going to France, has importuned me for a letter of introduction to you, which though I am but very little acquainted with him I could not refuse after making every reasonable apology. His views I am a stranger to. I am happy in the opportunity of thanking you for your kindness to Mr. Collas when a prisoner and in France. Mamma was well three weeks ago. The gentleman is waiting, and I have only time to assure you of my filial regard and that I am with respect, veneration, and love, your ever affectionate and dutiful niece."

Jane Mecom, actually in Rhode Island when her daughter wrote this letter for Thayer, came to Cambridge in October, met Thayer, and was interested in him because he told her of her brother's *Political, Miscellaneous, and Philosophical Pieces,* which had been published in London two years before without her ever hearing of it. On the twenty-third she wrote Thayer a letter of introduction to take to Franklin. "Mr. John Thayer, the gentleman by whom this goes, has had a liberal education and has served in this commonwealth with acceptance, but now chooses to go abroad with a view of seeing the world and making his fortune. I have no personal acquaintance with him, but hear he is much esteemed in Boston. I take the liberty to introduce him to my dear Brother, in hopes this one at least of seven letters I have wrote him since the date of his last to me that I have received, will reach his hand."

Six days later she wrote again, from Boston, to rejoice in the news of Yorktown and to say: "I wrote from Cambridge where my daughter lives by a young man who I expected was to sail the next day. I am afraid you will think me too presuming to introduce to you persons I know nothing of but by hearsay, but I am too apt to give way to their solicitations, and by that means have been troublesome to you, though I hope your long experience will enable you to get rid of them if they prove so." Jane had probably learned in Boston that Jonathan Williams, Sr., refused to give Thayer a letter of introduction to Franklin.

Patience Wright's son Joseph, the painter, returned to Boston late in 1782 and told Jane Mecom that not only was Franklin suffering severely from the stone but he had been annoyed by Thayer's impudent and demanding conduct. The story that Thayer insisted on being made chaplain to Franklin and the American legation seems to go back to Wright, though it is hard to substantiate. In any case, Franklin, well or sick, was as able as his sister supposed to get rid of troublesome applicants for his favor. But Jane Mecom, full of grief over her brother's bodily pain, could hardly bear the thought that she had perhaps made it worse by introducing Thayer to him. "It was Mrs. Wright's son," she wrote on December 26, "who told me of your sickness and of what mortified me very much besides, the condition and behavior of that—I had almost said—worthless little animal Thayer. I sincerely ask your pardon for introducing him to you, and have no other excuse but to tell you he took me in by being the first that informed me of a book that contained all your philosophical and political papers, and running on so prettily on one thing and another contained in them that I thought he must be clever. Tell me you forgive me and I will take more care for the future."

Franklin, who easily got rid of Thayer, was not troubled when he heard that the young man had gone to Rome and become a Roman Catholic in May 1783, and had come or was coming back to Paris to study for the priesthood. Protestant Boston was outraged, but to Franklin all religions or sects that made men virtuous were true and equal. If he thought lightly of Thayer, so did the Papal Nuncio in Paris, who on July 1, 1784, told Franklin that Thayer ought not to go to America to convert his countrymen, because "he knew nothing yet of his new religion himself." On that same day the Nuncio told Franklin that the Pope had, on the philosopher's recommendation, made John Carroll of Maryland "superior of the Catholic clergy in America, with many of the powers of a bishop": more precisely, prefect-apostolic. He five years later became the first Roman Catholic bishop in America.

Franklin, who lived a few months after Thayer returned to New England as a missionary of his new faith, might have guessed that the convert would, as he did, get on badly with Protestant public and Catholic authorities alike; but not that he would, in time, succeed as a missionary in Limerick and do much to encourage immigration from Catholic Ireland to his native Boston and other parts of America. At one time or another Franklin said various cheerful things about the loss of a Presbyterian to Rome, but nothing more cheerful, and possibly more prophetic, than what he wrote to Jane Mecom on September 13, 1783.

"Tell my Cousin Collas that the parson she recommended

to me is gone to Rome, and it is reported has changed his Presbyterianism for the Catholic religion. I hope he got something to boot, because that would be a sort of proof that they allowed our religion to be, so much at least, better than theirs. It would be pleasant, if a Boston man should come to be Pope! Stranger things have happened."

A Letter from You Once a Month

THE last letter Franklin wrote to America from France was to Jane Mecom. Since his resignation of his post as minister plenipotentiary, he was the most celebrated private citizen in the world. At St. Germain, twelve miles from Paris, he wrote on July 13, 1785, that he had set out "yesterday afternoon, and am here on my way to Havre de Grace, a seaport, in order to embark for America. I make use of one of the king's litters carried by mules, who walk steadily and easily, so that I bear the motion very well. I am to be taken on board a Philadelphia ship on the coast of England (Captain Truxtun) the beginning of next month. . . . As I may not have another opportunity before my arrival in Philadelphia (if it please God I do arrive), I write these particulars to go by way of England, that you may be less uneasy about me. I did my last public act in this country just before I set out, which was signing a treaty of amity and commerce with Prussia. I have continued to work till late in the day; 'tis time I should go home, and go to bed. . . . Though going to my own country, I leave this with regret, having received so much kindness in it, from all ranks of people. Temple and Benjamin [Bache] are with me, and send their dutiful respects."

The letter was sent to the New England Coffee House in London "to go per first ship," but it did not reach Jane Mecom till after Franklin's next to her, the first he wrote from Philadelphia after his arrival there. "I arrived here last Wednesday," he told her on September 19, "with my two grandsons and Cousin Jonathan Williams," the younger, "all well, thanks to God. . . . I am continually surrounded by congratulating friends, which prevents my adding more." She had to hear from other sources about the immense welcome he had in Philadelphia, and the instant demands on him for further service to the public.

Before she could receive this letter, the news of his return and of his state of health had got to Boston, and she sent him on the twenty-third her exultant greeting. "Blessed be God Who has brought my dear Brother safe to his desired port, That has answered my daily prayers for his comfort and ease, that you have had so good a passage and but one day's illness from the malady that attends you! I can never be thankful enough for these particulars, nor for His continual mercies to me, which are all along beyond my conception as well as deserts. I long so much to see you that I should immediately seek for some one that would accompany me and take a little care of me, but my daughter is gone into the country to git a little better, and I am in a strait between two; but the comfortable reflection that you are at home among all your dear children, and no more seas to cross, will be constantly pleasing to me till I am permitted to enjoy the happiness of seeing and conversing with you."

She had been in Rhode Island the past summer, she told him. "Our friend Catharine Greene is the same kind, good-natured creature she ever was (and so indeed is the Governor and all the family). She bids me never forget to remember her to you when I write. You will forgive all omissions and defects, as I fear the post will be gone before I can git it there," to the post office, "and can only add, God bless you all together forever, prays your affectionate sister."

On October 1 Franklin wrote that he had received her "kind letter. I should be happy to see you here, but cannot think of allowing you to take such a journey for that purpose, as I hope in the spring to be able to visit Boston."

On that same day Jane wrote to him again. "I can't express to you how much joy I feel at knowing you are at home and so much more at ease than I expected, in regard to your bodily state, but I perceive by the newspapers you are not to be suffered to rest as long as you live." The newspapers informed her that her brother had been nominated for a seat in the Supreme Executive Council of Pennsylvania. "I was in hopes you would have resolutely resisted all solicitations to burden yourself any more with the concerns of the public, and flattered myself if I were with you I should enjoy a little familiar domestic chitchat like common folks. But now I imagine all such attempts would be intrusion, and I may as well content myself at this distance with the hopes of receiving once in a while a kind letter from you, and believing you are happy with your other connections."

On the nineteenth, after she had read his letter telling her she must not undertake the long journey but that he hoped to come to Boston, she answered that now she "was satisfied, and will hope too that I shall see you in the spring; as it was before what I utterly despaired of, yet thoughts of your enjoying so much ease as to hope it will cheer many a gloomy hour I should otherways [have] had through the winter. . . . Be assured, my dear Brother, that there is not a day passes that my heart does not overflow with gratitude to you, and adoration of the Supreme Benefactor of all mankind Who puts in your power not only to make me as happy as humanity can expect to be, but enables you to diffuse your benefits, I had almost said, to the whole universe."

She hoped that Franklin would send her the catalogue of "the books you design for Franklin Town. My reason for this request is I have a great deal of time on my hands. I love reading. It is a present amusement, though my memory is so bad that I cannot retain it as many others do. Now I am sure that will be a collection worth reading, and I don't doubt I can borrow of one and another of my acquaintance from time to time such as I have a mind to read."

It was too good to seem true, after the long months of delay during the nine long years he had been in France, that letters could now go back and forth so rapidly between brother and sister. On October 27 he answered her letter of the nineteenth. "You shall have a copy of the catalogue of books as soon as I can find it; but you will see it sooner in the hands of Cousin Williams, to whom the books were consigned. Those you recommended of Dr. Stennett are among them." She had been associated in the gift with the Franklin whose name the town would hereafter bear.

Quietly telling her that, her brother with delicate tact proposed things she might do in her lonely winter ahead: things which would be helpful to him. Jonathan Williams, Jr., was bringing this letter to Boston. Though Franklin did not tell her, Jonathan had lost, not made, his fortune in France, and now wished to learn how to make crown soap; "and I promised him a copy of the receipt you were once so good as to write for me; but in my absence it is lost with many other of my papers. You will oblige me by writing it over again for me, but more by making a parcel for me of forty or fifty pounds weight, which I want for presents to friends in France who very much admired it. Jonathan will be glad to assist you (for the instruction's sake) in the working part. I wish it to be of the greenish sort that is close and solid and hard like the specimen I send; and not that which is white and curdled and crumbly."

Jane, reading these words from Benjamin, must have felt in every sentence the pleasure he so deftly intended. He was as proud as ever, she saw, of the crown soap which gave the Boston Franklins some claim to be remembered. She was the only one of them left who knew how to make it. Her brother had made it known to those great persons who were his friends in France. Though Jonathan was to help her, he would be profited by learning the art, and his young energy would be nothing without her skill. The specimen her brother sent was one of the cakes Jane had made at Catharine Greene's house, cherished by him for at least five years. And there was still another compliment to her in the postscript, again put in the form of a request for her help. "When you have a little leisure, write me an account of all the relations we have left in New England." This would be almost as good as talking with Benjamin about the father and mother and brothers and sisters they had so long survived: "familiar domestic chitchat like common folks."

Before Franklin's letter could reach her she wrote again, on November 7, to assure her brother that she was happy. "I live very much to my liking. I never had a taste for high life, for large companies and entertainments. I am of Pope's mind, that health, peace, and competence come as near to happiness as is attainable in this life, and I am in a good measure in possession of all three at present. If they are at times infringed occasionally, or by accident, I view it as the common lot of all and am not much disturbed.

"Our friend Catharine Greene expressed such lively joy at

the news of your arrival that her children told her it had
thrown her into hysterics, but she says she is not subject to
that disorder. She tells me you have honored them with a letter."

Jane's letter, she said, would be brought to Philadelphia
by "a gentleman who has connections with Mr. Bache, going
directly there." She had dined with the gentleman at the house
of Samuel Bradford, son-in-law to Jonathan Williams, Sr.,
"and ventured to invite him to come and drink tea with us,
which he readily accepted; and very politely offered to carry
your letter. We live always clean and look decent, and I
wanted he should tell you he saw me at home. My daughter
has returned from the country much mended in her health.
Her husband is expected every day from the West Indies; has
a prospect of doing better than common if he gits in safe.
She and my granddaughter Jenny Mecom remember their
duty to you."

By November 30 Jonathan Williams, Jr., was in Boston
"with the catalogue, for which I thank you," she wrote, "and
shall with pleasure comply with all you desire." She and
Jonathan had set up the leaches for the soap, and would make
it next week. "I am pleased that it will not totally die. I have
no stamp, and I fancy if any should be made for America it
would be clever to have thirteen stars; for the crown soap
now vended among us is as contemptible as the British head
that now wears one—dirty, stinking stuff. . . . I have begun
the account of our relations and shall send it in my next."

She had a favor she could not well avoid asking of her
powerful brother. "There is in your jail a young man, son to
Mr. [Nathaniel] Oliver of Chelsea who is dead, who is con-
demned for an assault. He has neither friends or relations
there. His father died poor, but he has a brother [Daniel]

who has worked himself, with the help of charity, through Dartmouth College and is now studying divinity. I have been many years acquainted with his grandmother on his mother's side, a worthy woman but in low circumstances and now near expiring with the palsy. I suppose on the strength of that he thought he might make application to me. He says his brother writes him he is perfectly innocent of the crime laid to his charge. . . . They think you can do everything, and I know you will do everything that is proper and convenient for you to do, but I very much fear the impropriety of my giving you the trouble of so much as reading this account of the matter. . . . I know nothing of the lad. He may deserve a halter for all I know, notwithstanding his being a branch of a good family."

By the end of December she had made sixty pounds of crown soap and was sending it to Philadelphia. It was "good and solid, but not so high a green color" as the specimen he sent her. She wished it were better.

On January 1, 1786, Franklin wrote her: "Our good God has brought us old folks, the last survivors of seventeen brothers and sisters, to the beginning of a new year. The measure of health and strength we enjoy at so advanced an age, now near fourscore, is a great blessing. Let us be cheerful and thankful."

Franklin was sorry that Jonathan Williams, Sr., had been in bad health. "I am glad to hear he is better, that your daughter is mended, and your son-in-law has good prospects. Young Oliver's fine was remitted before my arrival, but he lay in jail for his fees. He is now, as I hear, discharged. . . .

"Send me the name of the street you live in, that I may direct my letters so as not to give Cousin W. any trouble. My love to him and his family, and to yours." Franklin had known the Unity Street house for seventy years, and had owned it for almost thirty. But the names of the minor streets in Boston were so seldom used that he had to ask what the name of Jane's street was. She herself had to ask the neighbors, and it was six weeks before she had an answer. "My next-door neighbor, Mr. [Henry] Roby, calls it Clough Street; the Register for 1784 calls it Eliot Street; but another neighbor, Mr. [Jedidiah] Parker, who was brought up in it, says the records of his deeds call it Unity Street, which I believe must be right."

On January 6, before she got his New Year's letter, she wrote him that she wanted much to know about his health, but feared to be "too often inquisitive lest I should provoke you to return me such an answer as Chesterfield did to his son's widow on such an occasion, which would break my heart. I remember you once bade me not be fussy. Forgive. I won't think it possible."

What the Earl of Chesterfield had said to his son's widow was: "Upon my word, Madam, you interest yourself in the state of my existence more than I do myself, for it is worth the care of neither of us. I ordered my *valet de chambre*, according to your orders, to inform you of my safe arrival here; to which I can add nothing, being neither better nor worse." Jane did not say how or when she had come upon this incident in her reading, which was evidently wider than might have been expected.

She was glad, she told her brother, that the "poor young lad in jail" was "cleared and on his way home." Now she had another application to make. "By the recommendation of a couple of old women like myself, Mrs. [Dudson] Kilcup," whose husband had been a witness to John Franklin's will thirty years before, "and Mrs. Church, I was solicited to beg

your assistance to a poor woman whose husband was killed
in [Esek] Hopkins's fleet; was a second lieutenant; his name
was Philip Gaudin; has much due to her; the agents she says
is at Philadelphia. I evaded it as much as I could, but I don't
know but she will come again when she has got all her vouchers ready. All that are in trouble and know I am your sister
seem to think I can do something for them, so that you must
give me some directions how to proceed . . . or I shall always be in pain on such application and think you will be
afraid to receive a letter from me for fear of being teased.

"I have two favors to ask of you now: your new alphabet
of the English language and the *Petition of the Letter Z.*" The
Petition she had apparently heard of from Jonathan Williams,
Jr., and knew it was another of her brother's hoaxes, this time
at the expense of Ralph Izard who had spoken ill of Franklin.

At the end of her letter she took courage to put in a paragraph of sisterly protest: "I rejoice in every honorable mention that is made of you, but I cannot find it in my heart to
be pleased at your accepting the government of the state,"
as President of the Supreme Executive Council of Pennsylvania, in effect the governor; "and therefore have not con-
gratulated you on it. I fear it will fatigue you too much."

Franklin, replying on January 24, thanked her for "the receipt for making crown soap, which is very clearly written
. . . as well as for the account of our relations in New England," now lost. His health, he said, was "much the same as it
has been for some years past. The pains caused sometimes by
the stone do not augment, my appetite continues good, and
my temper generally cheerful; my strength and activity dimin-
ishing indeed, but by slow degrees. I don't know what the answer was which Chesterfield gave to his son's widow. . . .

"I have received a letter from the widow you mention as

having had a husband killed in Hopkins's fleet, but she has
sent me no vouchers on which I might found an application
in her favor, and I am afraid she has no other proof of the fact
but a *strong persuasion,* as she tells me, 'he was in the fleet
as sure as I am now alive, and lost his life in their cause'; and
afterwards says, 'I have waited near eight years in hopes that
he was taken and would return, but now my hopes are all fled;
that he fell a victim in their cause I *have not the least doubt.*'
It is strange that in eight years she has not been able to learn
whether he was killed or not; and as the Congress long since
appointed commissioners to examine and settle the claims of
persons or the representatives of persons who had served in
their ships or armies, which commissioners are doubtless
provided with muster rolls of the several corps, I wonder at
her not having applied directly to them.

"But there are people in the world, I have met with many
such, who love to have a kind of pocket complaint, always
at hand, with which they endeavor to procure compassion, by
exhibiting it everywhere and to everybody but those whose
proper business it would be to redress it. These they avoid, lest
their darling complaint, being examined, should be found to
have no foundation. I have written an answer to her letter,
which I enclose." The records of the Continental Navy do not
show that Gaudin was on any of Hopkins' ships; he was only
on a Massachusetts privateer.

"If you should have any future applications of this sort
made to you to be handed to me," Franklin said to his sister's
request for directions, "I think you may avoid giving yourself any trouble with them by acquainting the people that
I was absent all the war, must be unacquainted with the facts,
am now at a distance from Congress," then sitting in New
York, "have at present no connection with that body; and

that the application is more proper to be made to the delegates from their own state than to me."

He would send her when he could, he said, his new alphabet, the phonetic one he had invented in London and printed in the volume of 1779 which John Thayer had told her about. "*The Petition of Z* is enclosed. It should not be made public."

At the end he slyly countered her disapproval of his becoming President of Pennsylvania. "I do not wonder at your blaming me for accepting the government. We have all of us wisdom enough to judge what others ought to do, or not to do, in the management of their affairs; and 'tis possible I might blame you as much if you were to accept the offer of a young husband. My example may teach you not to be too confident in your own prudence; as it teaches me not to be surprised at such an event should it really happen."

To this last she replied on February 21, with no notice of his impudent talk about a new husband for her. "I ask your pardon if I appeared to blame you for accepting the government. I knew you must have had wise and good reasons for your conduct, but I feared the consequence of so close attention as appeared to me to be necessary in this difficult situation of affairs. May God give you help and prosperity!"

For some reason she never commented on the *Petition of the Letter* Z, a finished little hoax which punned on Ralph Izard's name and the variant *izzard* by which the letter *z* was sometimes known. The *Petition*, in which the letter solemnly complained about being put at the foot of the alphabet, was accompanied in the copy Franklin sent with a marginal gloss identifying izzard with Izard. "He was always talking," the gloss ran, "of his family and of his being a man of fortune, and complaining of his being treated, not with due respect, at the tail of the commission of ministers. He was not of the

commission for France, A. Lee being preferred to him, which
made him very angry; and the character here given of *s*," as
a "little, hissing, crooked, serpentine, venomous letter," "is
just what he in his passion gave Lee." Izard was, the gloss
said, "the most impatient man alive." Franklin said nothing
in the *Petition* of Izard's having abused his chief in Paris, only
of the abuse of Lee, who abused Franklin too. Jane Mecom
did not make the *Petition* public, and her copy with the only
known gloss accompanying it was not printed for more than
a century and a half after her death.

As for Mrs. Gaudin, she had given Jane, Jane wrote, "a
more plausible story than she appears to have given you. I
advised her not to write till she could git all the necessary
vouchers. Poor woman, I believe she had none, and is much
in the condition you describe." After that, Jane was more careful about sending her brother applications from strangers.

II

She was embarrassed as well as distressed when an ap-
plicant for Franklin's patronage turned up in her own family.
This was her grandson Josiah Flagg, now twenty-five, still
lame in one leg, and determined not to work at the trade he
had learned but instead to find what his aunt Jane Collas
called a more "genteel" occupation.

When Franklin returned from France, Josiah had left Massachusetts and was in Petersburg, Virginia. That was, he
wrote to Franklin in January 1786, no place for an ambitious
young man, and he hoped his uncle might help him find a
clerkship in Philadelphia. Franklin, ready to do anything that
would please his sister, wrote favorably to Josiah, but did
not mention him to Jane Mecom. She learned what Josiah had

done from Jonathan Williams, Jr., who may have had it from
Jane Collas, Josiah's correspondent in Boston. At the end of
February 1786 Jane Mecom wrote to her brother.

"Cousin Jonathan has just now informed me that my grandson Josiah Flagg has applied to you to put him into business.
Though he is my grandson and I wish him well settled to
something he can git his living by, I am angry with him for
his audacity in writing to you on such an account. He is a
poor unfortunate youth by having had a fall in his childhood
(made him lame in one knee) that disenables him for most
sorts of business, and has too proud a spirit to conform to the
occupation he was taught; and what his capacity is for any
other I am not qualified to inform you, though I am his grandmother. He has been at so great a distance from me ever since
the war commenced. But in answer to all my inquiries I have
always heard he behaved honestly and uprightly, and he has
appeared so when he has been to see me; but has had so
few advantages that it must be the highest impropriety in
him to address you on such an occasion."

Single-hearted in her desire to protect her brother from
any added burden, Jane was unjust to her grandson, who was
handicapped not only by his lameness but also by the inse-
curity bred in him by his early years of dependence on relatives. "I was left a helpless orphan at fourteen," he later wrote,
"and during the whole Revolution suffered very much." He
was self-educated, and somewhat affected and pretentious
as a young man, but hardly to be blamed for leaving a trade
he did not like and looking for a livelihood more suited to his
tastes, and indeed to his capacities.

On April 17 Josiah Flagg wrote from Philadelphia to his
"Dear Grandma. I have the pleasure," he said, "to inform you
of my safe arrival in this city from Virginia after a passage

of fourteen days, which in good weather is accomplished in three. Prior to my intention of visiting this place I wrote my Uncle Franklin, and he was kind enough to honor me with a favorable answer. I was introduced to him by Captain Robinson, a citizen of Philadelphia who came passenger with me, and was received in a very cordial and affectionate manner. I expect to be employed in writing for him three or four months, and if you would use your influence with him in a recommendation of me, it may perhaps be attended with favorable consequences. I endeavor to behave as well as my slender education and knowledge of the world will admit. No man's abilities are so remarkably shining as not to stand in need of the praises of a friend, a patron, and even a proper opportunity to recommend them to the notice of the world.

"If you will be kind enough to point out to His Excellency my good intentions, and the character which I have ever sustained, unblemished, it may have a pleasing effect. I was candid with him in telling of my indigent circumstances, but I never told him I spun out three years under the patronage of St. Crispin," that is, as a shoemaker or shoemaker's apprentice, "and I humbly beg you'd omit that in your letter to him.

"Dear Grandma, now is the time for me to appear to the best advantage, and your kind assistance will confer a peculiar favor on your ever dutiful grandson."

His grandmother at once wrote Josiah a severe letter, now missing, and sent it along with one to Franklin, to whom she said: "I am sorry you are, as it were, forced to bear the burden of supporting my whole family. . . . I think it was disrespectful in him to me not to ask my advice, but as he has now desired my recommendation I will enclose you his letter to me, wherein you will see the man as he is, and I can add nothing to it, as it contains all I believe about him." She had no scruple at giving away Josiah's secret about his former trade, which she thought he had no right or excuse to keep from Franklin. "He has, as I think, thrust himself rudely under your protection. I however thank you for your notice of him, and hope he will so behave as to obtain your future approbation. I know your wisdom and goodness will incline you to watch over and admonish, or reprove, him, as you find occasion, and if you can make him ashamed of that ridiculous vanity he so much indulges, and convert him from it, you may by that means save a soul from death and hide a multitude of sins. I don't wish him to know I sent you his letter, and if you have a convenient opportunity, please to send it back." This Franklin forgot or neglected to do, and the letter is still among his papers.

By the time Jane signed her letter to Franklin she was less angry, and she was kinder in a postscript: "I believe I have written too severe to poor Josiah, and as he is among all strangers and so much his superiors, it may depress his spirits; and I really think him a good young man in the main. I know no fault he has but his vanity. You will know whether he wants encouragement, and your goodness will administer it in the properest way. I should be sorry to have him take a disgust at his old Grandmother, and I must send these [letters] or none as the vessel is just going."

Josiah remained on her conscience, and appeared in all her letters to Philadelphia during May. "I thank you," she wrote her brother, "for employing him. Writing he appears to me to be well qualified for; and with your permission he may in the meantime learn many valuable things by being near you and making observations. And I beg, my dear Brother, you will as far as you can, without interfering with your other affairs, inspect his conduct, his disposition, and his capacity,

and reprove, advise, and direct him in what you see to be
most proper for him: which if he does not observe he need
not expect prosperity any way. He is, to be sure, as destitute
of friends capable of assisting him as almost any one. I hope
he will do well. My love to him."

Again: "If you have a little leisure, it will oblige me very
much to hear from you something about my grandson, where
he lives, how he behaves, what company he keeps, and what
you think of him. He is the son of a dear worthy child; his
sister [Jane Flagg Greene] was remarkably dutiful and affectionate to me; and I wish him well, but should never have
consented to his throwing himself upon you. Therefore, he
has acted as those who are called the wise of this world are
apt to do, to endeavor to make himself a friend of one who
is able to help him, and if he so behaves as to be worthy of
your notice I shall not be sorry he did not ask my advice."

And yet again, to Sarah Bache: "Where does my poor
grandson live? For, though my brother has been so good
as to permit him to be there and to employ him for the present,
I know your house is too small and your family too large,
to find room for him there, and I hope he is in no way troublesome to you."

Early in June Franklin quietly put his sister at ease on the
subject of Josiah, who did live in the same house with his
uncle and the Baches. "Your grandson behaves very well,
and is constantly employed in writing for me, and will be so
some time longer. As to my reproving and advising him, which
you desire, he has not hitherto appeared to need it, which is
lucky, as I am not fond of giving advice, having seldom seen
it taken. An Italian poet in his account of a voyage to the
moon tells us that

All things lost on earth are treasured there.

On which somebody observed, there must be in the moon a great deal of *good advice.*" Franklin, hinting that his sister was perhaps too zealous in giving advice, no more bothered to say it in so many words than he bothered to name the Italian poet as Ariosto, of whom Jane would probably not have heard.

Josiah wrote a long letter and two short ones, all missing, to his grandmother before she answered him, in July. She was kind now, but she still believed in giving advice and gave him more of it.

"I have received your long letter and read it many times, and never without tears; by which you may see that I am not without affectionate feelings towards you. But I have always made it my practice in my conduct towards my first children to reprove and advise when it appeared to me to be necessary, and I still persist in the belief of its being proper and useful . . . and I hope what I wrote to you has not been of any real prejudice to you. You may assure yourself it proceeded from a sincere desire of your best good, and [I] shall always rejoice at whatever turns out to your comfort or advantage.

"I much approve of your conduct in not making acquaintance while you remain in that family. Your reasons are very judicious. If you can but look on the time you spend in that retired manner as a school in which you are to acquire experience and judgment to govern your future life, it will pass with less reluctance. May you go on and hold out in the principles you appear now to act from, and God bless you and prosper you!

"By no means suffer yourself to despond, and particularly on account of the loss of [the use of] your leg. Was Mr. Pratt the lawyer ever respected the less by sensible people for the loss of his?" Josiah could hardly have seen Benjamin Pratt,

a distinguished Boston lawyer who for a time was chief justice
of New York, but the lame child must have been told that
Mr. Pratt too had only one good leg and went on crutches.

"I acknowledge," the grandmother said, "what I wrote
concerning veracity had such an appearance as you suppose,
but could not conveniently alter the terms at that time. I own
I had no other cause than the request you then made me"—
to keep from Franklin the fact that Josiah had worked as a
shoemaker—"which, besides its not being agreeable to my
judgment, was then out of my power to comply with, for I
had already wrote" to Franklin "concerning it. But now all
is well and I hope you will try for the future, if you can *honestly* write 'affectionate' as well as 'dutiful grandson.' . . . I
am and ever was your affectionate grandmother."

In September Josiah arrived at his grandmother's house
in Boston with a certificate, written in his own hand but signed
by Franklin. "This is to certify whom it may concern, that
Josiah Flagg has lived with me near five months, being employed as a clerk and accountant, and has behaved with great
ability, diligence, and fidelity, so as to give me perfect satisfaction. . . . This testimony is given unasked." His certificate
and his experience gave Josiah his opportunity. He returned
to Lancaster, Massachusetts, married, had six children (one
of them named George Washington), served as town clerk
for many years, and, when he died at seventy-nine, left the
town books adorned with his excellent penmanship.

III

Josiah Flagg, anxiously trying to keep his shoemaking past
from his uncle, who knew of it, must have wondered at Franklin's pride and delight in crown soap, that reminder of his

own boyhood drudgery. Here was the celebrated philosopher, President of the Supreme Executive Council of Pennsylvania, sending a box of "our soap . . . thought to be the best in the world for shaving and for washing chintzes and other things of delicate colors" to his friends in France: to his dear friends Madame Helvétius and Madame Brillon, the neighbors Chaumont and Le Veillard of Passy, the worldly Abbés de la Roche, Morellet, and Arnaud, the scientists Cabanis and Le Roy, the bankers Grand, and the young girl, daughter of Chaumont, whom Franklin smilingly called his wife.

Or here was Franklin writing his sister about an experiment he and his daughter had made with some of the soap that had crumbled as it dried. "Sally . . . put three or four pound of the crumbs, about the size of chestnuts, in a little kettle with water, and over a slow fire melted them together, and when the whole was uniformly fluid, laded it out into little paper pans of the size of the cakes. These grew stiff when cold, but were rather soft and shrunk greatly in drying. Being now dry, they are exceedingly hard, close-grained, and solid, and appear to have all the qualities of excellent crown soap, only in drying they are twisted and warped out of shape; wherefore I have not continued the process, but resolved to send you this particular account, thinking you may possibly teach me a better method."

Jane had never had any such experience with the soap, but she told him that in a new lot she was making she had used twelve pounds of wax to twenty of tallow, which might improve the consistency. More discussion went back and forth between brother and sister about their efforts to revive a lost art. "There is a good deal of philosophy in the working of crown soap that I don't understand," she had to admit late in May.

Franklin, telling her of his and Sally's experiment, asked his sister to "draw upon me for the expense of the soap, and your bill shall be paid on sight." And she replied: "My dear good gentleman, how could you mention my drawing on you for the cost of a little soap, when all I enjoy is of your bounty? I could not help crying when I read it. The pleasure I enjoy in the hope of gratifying you is a full compensation." He did not argue with her: "Since you will not let me pay you for it, accept at least my thanks, which indeed you had merited by your readiness to oblige me, even if you had allowed me to reimburse you."

"I really think myself highly favored," she wrote in August, "in receiving a letter from you once a month, as I have for three past. It is indeed a short space of time to what I used to suffer in anxiety." In that year, 1786, she exchanged more letters with him than in any other of their lives. At times the letters overlapped in date and subject, but now and then their correspondence amounted almost to conversation.

On April 8 he wrote her that their old friend Captain All, just arrived in Philadelphia from Boston, had "given me the pleasure of hearing that you were very well a few weeks since; he says he does not remember you to have ever looked better, or to be more active."

"I am obliged to Captain All," she wrote on the twenty-second, "for giving you such a favorable idea of your sister. The truth is, when I am in agreeable company it raises my spirits and might then have some influence on my activity; and for the greatest part of my time, when I am sitting at home, I am apt to imagine as Samson did when he lost his hair, that I can arise and shake myself and go forth as at other times. But on trial, like him, I am woefully disappointed, and find my feet crippling and my breath short; but I am still cheerful, for that is my natural temper, and am, as you advise me, thankful that I escape many grievous calamities incident to old age—and that my dear brother does not grow worse of his."

In that same letter she said in a postscript: "I know there is few words spelt right, and it is miserable blotted, but my dear brother will excuse it as I have not time to correct it."

About this, and other apologies of the sort, Franklin wrote her on July 4 his most famous comment on the spelling of English: "You need not be concerned in writing to me, about your bad spelling; for in my opinion, as our alphabet now stands, the bad spelling, or what is called so, is generally the best, as conforming to the sound of the letters and of the words. To give you an instance: A gentleman receiving a letter in which were these words, 'Not finding Brown at hom, I delivered your meseg to his yf,' the gentleman finding it bad spelling, and therefore not very intelligible, called his lady to help him read it. Between them they picked out the meaning of all but the 'yf,' which they could not understand. The lady proposed calling her chambermaid; 'for Betty,' says she, 'has the best knack at reading bad spelling of any one I know.' Betty came, and was surprised that neither Sir nor Madam could tell what 'yf' was. 'Why,' says she, ' "yf" spells "wife." What else can it spell?' And indeed it is a much better as well as shorter method of spelling 'wife' than by *doubleyou, i, ef, e,* which in reality spells 'doubleyifey.' ' "

"I think Sir and Madam," Jane commented in reply, "were deficient in sagacity that they could not find out 'yf' as well as Betty, but sometimes the Bettys has the brightest understanding."

The volume containing Franklin's "proposal of a new alphabet" came to Boston by water, and was slow in reaching Jane

Mecom. She called the frontispiece "your profile done more to your likeness than any I have heretofore seen," and at once went to work to master his "Scheme for a new Alphabet and reformed Mode of Spelling." As to spelling in the traditional mode, she was, she said, "but one of the thousands and thousands that write on to old age and can't learn." She could read the sentences printed in the new alphabet, but found the phonetic letters hard to form, and seemed not to understand that the words, however spelled, were to be pronounced the same as before. He wrote no more about it, and she soon forgot the matter, or at least let it drop.

In his letter of July 4 Franklin said: "There is much rejoicing in town today, it being the anniversary of the Declaration of Independence, which we signed this day ten years, and thereby hazarded lives and fortunes. God was pleased to put a favorable end to the contest much sooner than we had reason to expect."

And Jane Mecom on the twenty-first: "I perceive you have kept the 4th July very honorably as well as joyfully. We also observed as usual, but we had so lately celebrated the opening the bridge on Charles River, being a new thing, the other was not so much noticed in our papers. You will I hope next spring have the pleasure of seeing it yourself. It is really a charming place. They have leveled the rising ground that led to it and nicely paved it, that at some distance as you approach to it, it is a beautiful sight, with a little village at the other end, the buildings all new. The prospect on each side is delightful. I frequent[ly] go on the hill," Copp's Hill, not far from her house, "for the sake of the prospect and the walk. And if I tell you I have once walked over, I suppose you won't allow it as great a feat as your walking ten miles before breakfast, but I am strongly inclined to allow it myself, all circumstances considered. It is thought the toll gatherers received yesterday, being Commencement Day" at Harvard, "five hundred dollars. Perhaps it may be only an extravagant guess."

In August she seems to have been reading, in the volume he had sent her, his remarks on what would be a "sufficient conductor" to carry lightning from distributed points on a building to the ground. "We know," he there said, "of no instance where a complete conductor to the moist earth has been insufficient if half an inch diameter." This led to her one known reference to his most famous invention. "Our North Church folks," she wrote him, "are repairing their steeple, and it was thought the electrical wire was too small to conduct a large stroke of lightning. I felt uneasy about it, and got Mr. Collas to inquire about it; and he tells me they have made it three times as big as it was before."

She was on surer ground when she read his September letter, about the addition he was building to his house in Philadelphia. "I hardly know how," he said, "to justify building a library at an age that will soon oblige me to quit it; but we are apt to forget that we are grown old, and building is an amusement."

"To enlarge your present dwelling," she insisted, "will not only be an amusement, but in all probability a sample of many ingenious contrivances for others to profit by in future. . . . It is a favorable circumstance that you can sometimes forget you are grown old; otherwise it might check you in many useful discoveries you are making for your fellow men. I wish our poor distracted state," then in the early stages of Shays' rebellion, "would attend to the many good lessons which have been frequently published for their instruction; but we seem to want wisdom to guide, and honesty to comply with our duty, and so keep always in a flame."

Early in the fall Franklin wrote: "Some knowing ones here in matters of weather predict a hard winter. Permit me to have the pleasure of helping to keep you warm. Lay in a good stock of firewood, and draw upon me for the amount."

His gift was particularly welcome this year, she wrote back. Captain Collas, who "supplied us last year with twelve cords of wood, which lasted us till warm weather, as we kept but one fire except on some extraordinary occasions . . . has been so unsuccessful as to be now eight months out of business, and has spent what he had acquired before, that I believe he does not know now to git one cord without running in debt. . . . I was not anxious however, for I knew I could but ask for some of the principal of which I receive the interest, and supply all I want and very probably should have sufficient for the remainder of my life; but your goodness in offering the wood makes it needless to ask. Wood is now fourteen shillings a cord, and it will cost three shillings a cord to saw it and bring in.

"And I will now venture to tell you I wish for a load or two extraordinary to bestow on a poor family who are worthy objects of charity; but if you think this is too boldly pressing on your beneficence, like my putting my hand into your pocket to supply others' wants as well as my own, I will not think it hard to be denied.

"I will tell you the family and the circumstances. You may remember a man that made your sticcado when you were last in Boston, and his wife who had been my son Edward's widow." Poor Edward's widow, and her poorer second husband, Thomas Foot! "He has had the misfortune to be burst [ruptured], that he is not able to do the harder part of his occupation, which you may remember is a shop joiner or more properly cabinetmaker. But going out of town in the siege, he lost all his tools; they were somehow thrown overboard and could not be recovered. They lived in the country some years, she keeping school and he jobbing about till her health grew very infirm, and they were advised to come back to Boston—I suppose for fear they should become a charge to the town [Dunstable]. Here he works journey work and little matters in other men's shops as he is able, and she has done every kind of thing that she was able to git a living (and she is ingenious and industrious) till she grew so decrepit and infirm that for some years she has been almost entirely deprived of the use of her limbs, and they live mostly on the charity of friends; among whom I have not been altogether negligent of contributing my mite, but I think ought to be but a mite without your permission, on whose bounty I live." And in another letter soon afterwards: "You are so good you have never denied any request I made you. If you think I have presumed too far you will only laugh at it a little, but you must give me a caution not to make so free with you another time."

To so much her brother could do no more than reply with the least possible, which was: "I approve of the friendly disposition you made of some of your wood. I wish you a comfortable winter."

Franklin wrote that he had "lately received a letter from a person who subscribes himself Stickney; says he is a grandson of my Sister Davenport and has a son named Benjamin, to whom he desires to give a good education, but cannot well afford it. You have not mentioned this family in the list you sent me. Do you know anything of them?"

"Your predictions concerning a hard winter," she wrote him on December 17, "are beginning to be verified in a formidable manner. The snow has been so deep, and we no man in the house, that we might have been buried alive were it not for

the care of some good neighbors who began to dig us out before we were up in the morning; and Cousin Williams came
puffing and sweating as soon as it was possible to see how we
were and if we wanted anything. But thank God we had no
want of anything necessary if we had been shut up a fortnight—except milk." Grateful for the wood he had sent her,
she thanked him for the "charming barrel of flour" he had sent
as well.

Jane knew a good deal about the Stickneys, and on January
6, 1787, poured it out in a lively stream that must have been
like her spicier conversation when she was in agreeable company. "Our Sister Davenport," she said, "had a daughter
Dorcas who married to a Mr. [Captain Anthony] Stickney
and lived at Newbury. He was a chairmaker by trade, but
never loved work. But that is not the thing. They had been
so long dead, and I had no remembrance of their leaving any
children and had never seen any of them, that I suppose I did
not think of the family when I wrote the list. When I received
your letter our streets were unpassable by any means for old
folks; but a few days after I sent to Mrs. [Jonathan] Williams
[Sr.] to inquire what she knew about them; and had for answer, all she knew of the man who wrote to you was that he
was a good-for-nothing, impudent, lazy fellow just like his father. I thought however as he had an aunt in the town I would
know something farther before I answered your letter. I therefore got a carriage and went to her and inquired about the
family.

"She told me that when her sister was married her husband's mother and grandfather were living on a little estate
they had in Newbury, where he also carried his wife after
trying to live by shopkeeping in this town. But having so lit-

tle means of support they became exceeding poor, in which time she says you went to see them and made them a handsome present (I suppose at the time you put out your shoulder at Portsmouth). His grandfather lived to be above ninety year old, but he and his daughter dying left the house to our cousin [Dorcas Davenport's husband], but they could not feed long upon that. He therefore took a prudent step and bought a good farm at Derry, and went to live on it, where his wife helped to work and they got to live extraordinary well. But she, Mrs. Rogers thinks, shortened her days by too hard labor, and her husband died soon after her and left the farm to this man [the Anthony Stickney who had applied to Franklin] and his sister, who are all the children they left, and who live together on it and do very well. She [Mary Davenport Rogers, step-sister to Dorcas] says he has a good character as a sober, honest man, but does not increase his estate, as one told her he entertained too many strangers in hopes of entertaining angels unawares. She says she saw him about a year and a half ago, and he told her he had such a son that he named for you; but she thinks him very bold in writing to you. She is sure she should not have done it. As to the boy, I omitted to inquire particularly about him, as the carriage waited for me, put it out of my mind."

After a silence of three months Jane wrote again about the weather and the Stickneys. "I know it will be a pleasure to you to know that I have as good health as I could expect this most intolerable hard winter. Your prediction has held invariable this far, and as it began in October I don't see why it mayn't hold till May, for any appearance yet to the contrary. I have wanted nothing for my comfort but air and exercise, which it has been impossible for me to take; as the feet of

every woman, as well as the hand of every man, has been
sealed up. It is true I do walk sometimes in the house, but I
don't think of it often enough. . . .

"When I wrote you concerning our sister's grandson, I mis-
took the places of his abode. He lives at Chester, in the County
of Rockingham, State of New Hampshire. He has been to see
me the first time, though he is forty years old. Says how happy
he should be to have the honor of a letter from you, which I
believe would elevate the poor man to a high degree. He said
he was advised to write you concerning his son. I told him if
you were to take such notice of all who had been named in
respect to you, you must build an academy for their reception;
that I had a grandson [Franklin Greene] perhaps would claim
admittance when it was well established, though I had not
yet proposed it." Postscript: "Dear Brother, pardon the blots
and blunders. I can't make a [quill] pen myself and have no
one near me who can."

In Jane Mecom there were wells of gossip to which, with
her brother, she seldom gave outlet, as here about the Stickneys. She was more likely to do it with Sarah Bache, as in a
letter of May 1786. Jane sent her particular love to "my niece
Miss Betsey. . . . Tell her the pincushion she sent me is much
admired; but I question if it may ever be said of it what I
can tell you of the pocketbook you worked for your Grandmother Franklin when you were but five years old. It was
done in cross-stitch and was very beautiful. When my mother
died I gave it to Cousin Kezia Coffin, who admired it, and
always used it when she went abroad [away from home],
which was a great deal; and when it got soiled, she cleaned
it and bound it. The last time I saw her, which was since the
peace, she had it in her pocket; but it had been so much worn
that she had lined it with a piece of fine scarlet broadcloth,

and darned it down on that, and made it up so that it looked still quite bright and handsome. Tell Betsey hers shall be kept as long as I live."

On the day Jane Mecom wrote to her niece about the pincushion, she wrote to her brother, and no less truly in a language natural to her heart, about life now and to come. "I tell you these things that you may see I do enjoy life here. But truly, my dear Brother, I am willing to depart out of it whenever my Great Benefactor has no farther use for me. For though but little of that appears to me now, I know the most insignificant creature on earth may be made some use of in the scale of beings, may touch some spring or verge to some wheel unperceived by us. But Oh may I not live to hear of the departure of my dear Brother!"

The most touching communication between sister and brother in 1786 was words on one side and silence on the other. "I have seen Mr. [John] Vaughan," she wrote in late May, "and he gives me the satisfaction to hear you have not been so ill since you got home as to keep [to the] house on that account, though he does not give me any encouragement that you will be able to come to Boston. The spring is gone and I have no hopes now, but who knows but we may live to another spring? You not being worse, and perhaps eased of the care of government, may bless your friends this way with a visit. I love to hope the best." Franklin did not reply, and the two put off the visit to the spring of some other year.

10

Something to Wean Us
from This World

IN MAY 1787 Colonel Winthrop Sargent called on Jane
Mecom to tell her he was going to Philadelphia and would
gladly carry a letter from her to Dr. Franklin. She had heard
of her brother's appointment as a delegate from Pennsylvania
to the Federal Convention which was meeting to frame a new
Constitution for the United States. "I wanted to tell you," she
wrote, "how much pleasure I enjoy in the constant and lively
mention of you in the newspapers, which makes you appear
to me like a young man of twenty-five just setting out for the
other eighty years full of great designs for the benefit [of]
mankind, and your own nation in particular; which I hope
with the assistance of such a number of wise men as you are
connected with in the Convention you will gloriously accomplish, and put a stop to the necessity of dragooning and
haltering. They are odious means. I had rather hear of the
swords being beat into plowshares and the halters used for
cart ropes, if by that means we may be brought to live peace-
ably with one another."

Strange that Major William Pierce of Georgia, also a delegate to the Federal Convention, who first saw Franklin that
summer, should say of the "greatest philosopher of the present

age" that in spite of his many years he showed an "activity of mind equal to a youth of twenty-five": the soldier in Philadelphia agreeing so precisely with the sister in Boston. Franklin had called up all his perennial energy for his final great achievement.

The Convention submerged him, but on May 30, the day after the Convention adopted the rule of secrecy for its members and settled to work, Franklin wrote his sister his last letter for four months except two or three official notes on routine state or national affairs.

In the letter to Jane Mecom he said nothing about the Convention, but instead answered her questions about the addition to his house which had given him "a large cellar for wood, a drawing room or dining room on the same level with our old dining room, in which new room we can dine a company of 24 persons, it being 16 feet wide and 30½ long; and it has two windows at each end, the north and south, which will make it an airy summer room; and for winter there is a good chimney in the middle, made handsome with marble slabs. Over this room is my library, with like windows at each end, and lined with books to the ceiling." He accounted for the other space in the new addition and told her how it was entered from the original house. "All these rooms are now finished and inhabited very much to the convenience of the family, who were before too much crowded."

In August Jane spoke of her pleasure in hearing of his house. "If we may judge of the fitness of things, we may surely expect one who has employed his whole life to diffuse happiness to all the world, has a right to live in a commodious house, and that all about him should combine to promote his happiness." She spoke of the "lowly dwelling" in which they had passed their childhood. Now: "Blessed be God that you and *I*, by your means, have the addition of more pleasing appearance in our dwellings!" They had come a great way from the Blue Ball.

On September 20, three days after the adoption and signing of the Constitution, Franklin broke his long silence first with a letter to her. "The Convention finished the 17th instant," he told her. "I attended the business of it five hours in every day from the beginning"—not to mention that he was present on many of these days also at meetings of the Supreme Executive Council, which came often to meet at his house. "You may judge from thence," he went on, "that my health continues. Some tell me I look better, and they suppose the daily exercise of going and returning from the State House has done me good." Nothing here about being carried in his sedan chair, which he was careful never to mention to her, though she must have heard of it. "You will see the Constitution we have proposed in the papers. The forming of it so as to accommodate all the different interests and views was a difficult task; and perhaps after all it may not be received with the same unanimity in the different states that the Convention have given the example of in delivering it out for their consideration. We have however done our best, and it must take its chance.

"I agree with you perfectly in your disapprobation of war," he said, and made a famous comment on the wastefulness of war. He told her about the precautions he had taken to make his house fireproof; he closed with a thought of her for the winter ahead. "I sent you lately a barrel of flour, and I blame myself for not sooner directing you to lay in your winter's wood, and drawing upon me for it as last year. But I have been so busy. To avoid such neglect in the future, I now make the direction general, that you draw on me every year for the same purpose."

On November 4 he felt so well that he told her he had hoped he might "be at liberty to take a trip to Boston in the spring," but he now admitted he was continuing in office for another year. "I must own that it is no small pleasure to me, and I suppose it will give my sister pleasure that, after such a long trial of me, I should be selected a third time by my fellow-citizens, without a dissenting vote but my own, to fill the most honorable post in their power to bestow. This universal and unbounded confidence of a whole people flatters my vanity more than a peerage could do."

Before his letter could reach her, three letters were written to him from Boston. One on the eighth was from Catharine Greene. "I'm now on a visit," she said, "to your good sister, who I find very comfortable and as much in health as can expect for a person so far advanced. We have had a real feast on you. You may rejoice you was not between us, as we might possibly each took a piece. My stay is only three days in town, as we expect snow every day. I only came to Providence for a visit of a week, and the fine sunshine invited me here. I go from here today. The parting is painful, but you used to say if we did not go, we could not come again." She gave him news of the Boston cousins and of her own family at Warwick. "Heaven's best of blessings attend my much loved friend."

The next day Jane Mecom wrote, enclosing Catharine's letter. "Her affection for you is really so great that she seems at a loss to express it. The letters from us two old women, proceeding from such a cause, will be a variety and amuse you a little under the fatigue of public business."

Richard Bache's friend, a Mr. Wouters, had been several times to call in Unity Street and would bring the letters to Franklin. This gave Jane Collas an opportunity to write on the eleventh a third letter, of which her mother did not then know. "I can hold out no longer," Jane Collas began. "Madam Greene has been permitted to write you without one objection from my monopolizing Mamma; and if love can apologize for troubling you with one female letter, why not for another? No one breathing can plead a greater share than myself, and I have more than once shed tears on being denied the pleasure of telling you I love and reverence you even to adoration; and should I ever have the happiness of seeing you (though I would not bite a bit off you as Mrs. Gr——ne seems to long for), I would shove in among the crowd and, if possible, touch the hem of your garment. . . . I hope to slide this unperceived into the hand of the obliging Mr. Wouters, and do you not blame me, my dear Uncle, for disobedience to a parent, as we are only to obey them *in the Lord*, which I take to be conscientiously."

It had been difficult for Jane Collas, listening to her mother and her friend, not to resent their assumption that Franklin was theirs alone, with no younger woman admitted to correspondence with him. The mother was selfish and jealous, the friend from Rhode Island hardly better than a cannibal, Jane Collas felt. She had to get her word in by stealth. If it was not always easy for Jane Mecom to live with the languishing Jane Collas, neither was it for Jane Collas to live with the dominating Jane Mecom.

A month later Franklin wrote his sister some news that infuriated her. "Your son Collas has been here from North Carolina, where he kept a store, but it has not answered his expectations. He wanted to take up goods on credit here, but could not obtain any unless I would recommend it to our merchants to give it, which I could not do without making myself liable; and that I did not incline to do, having no opinion either of the honesty and punctuality of the people with whom he proposed to traffic or of his skill and acuteness in merchandising. I write this merely to apologize for any seeming unkindness on my part in not so promoting his views."

The visit of the irresponsible Captain Collas evidently made Franklin think again about his sister's affairs. "You always tell me," he said, "that you live comfortably; but I sometimes suspect that you may be too unwilling to acquaint me with any of your difficulties, from an apprehension of giving me pain. I wish you would let me know precisely your situation, that I may better proportion my assistance to your wants. Have you any money at interest, and what does it produce? Or do you do some kind of business for a living? If you have hazarded any of your stock in the above-mentioned trading project [Collas's], I am afraid you will have but slender returns. Lest you should be straitened during the present winter, I send you on a corner of this sheet a bill of exchange on our Cousin Tuthill Hubbart for fifty dollars, which you can cut off and present to him for payment."

To this letter Jane Mecom replied on January 8 with the most explicit paragraph she ever wrote about her daily life. "I have a good, clean house to live in, my granddaughter constantly to attend me to do whatever I desire in my own way and in my own time. I go to bed early, lie warm and comfortable, rise early to a good fire, have my breakfast directly and eat it with a good appetite, and then read or work or what else I please. We live frugally, bake all our own bread, brew small beer, lay in a little cider, pork, butter, etc., and supply ourselves with plenty of other necessary provision daily at the door," from farmers or tradesmen who went from house to house. "We make no entertainments, but sometimes an intimate acquaintance will come in and partake with us the dinner we have provided for ourselves and a dish of tea in the afternoon; and if a friend sits and chats a little in the evening we eat our hasty pudding (our common supper) after they are gone."

She had never wished to deceive him, but since his "penetrating eye" could discover "the smallest symptom and the remotest consequences," she at last summed up the history of Captain Collas—a history which was of late even shabbier than it had been. Dismissed for incompetence, if not worse, after his voyage to the West Indies, he spent all he had earned and obliged his mother-in-law to protect herself. "I thought it absolutely necessary to secure their necessary furniture lest it should be attached by some other creditor, and got him to make it over to me. He then run in debt to all who would trust him, and patched up this trading voyage; was to sell all and return in two months with the produce. . . . He stayed seven, made no remittances, sent his wife in the time a bill of twenty dollars, which if it was right she should receive she was cheated of. He, thinking she had received it, came home to help eat it, and brought another small bill but not a farthing returns for any of the adventurers"—that is, the other investors in the trading voyage.

"This being his case, I trembled at every knock at the door lest it should be some officer with demands on him. I at length told him he had no right to live without labor, any more than any other man. He was strong and able, and if he could not git to be master of a vessel he must go mate. He should not choose to do that neither. I told him the expenses of the family when he was at home were double to what they were when he was absent; and that if I continued to spend as I now did I should have naught for my own support. He acknowledged it all and went back to the same place. But the shameless impudence of the wretch to go to Philadelphia and make such application to you was beyond my conception."

About the time Jane Mecom wrote this letter her brother fell on the same stone steps, leading to his garden, down which she had fallen on her first visit to Philadelphia. It sprained his right arm and wrist so badly that he did not write her till April, and then only a brief note, telling her of the accident, and his recovery, and his health "in other respects." On the same day he wrote to Jane Collas, without a word about her husband. "As to my coming to Boston," he said, "which you seem to wish, and I also, I begin to doubt its being ever accomplished. Such a journey at my age would be attended with much inconvenience and hardship, and might, with the malady I have, be dangerous." To go would "give myself and my friends a good deal of trouble, which cannot be compensated by our pleasure of meeting since that will be balanced by the pain of parting."

At the end of May he wrote again to his sister. In a missing letter from her, he said, she mentioned her "sufferings last winter by imagining and foreboding that some sickness or misfortune had befallen me. It may not be amiss to allow ourselves beforehand the enjoyment of some expected pleasure, the expectation often being the greatest part of it; but it is not so well to afflict ourselves with apprehensions of misfortunes that may never arise. Death however is sure to come to us all, and mine cannot now be far off, being in my 83rd year. But that may be to me no misfortune, and I shall take care to make it as small a one to you as possible."

Franklin was then thinking about his will, signed six weeks

later, in which he left his "dear sister, Jane Mecom, a house and lot I have in Unity Street, Boston, now or late under the care of Mr. Jonathan Williams, to her and to her heirs and assigns forever," and also "the yearly sum of fifty pounds sterling, during life, to commence at my death." Once dead, he could no longer comfort her heart, but he could still safeguard her against poverty as long as she lived. If that was all he could do, it was the best he could do.

Jane, perhaps because the unanswerable, irreducible words of his letter seemed intolerably bleak to her, was so shocked by them that for a time she was in bewildered misery. "I see you are angry with me," she wrote three weeks later, "and I cannot bear my brother's displeasure. I am anxious for your life, it is true, but also for your sufferings here, as I had reason from my own experience of a fall from the same place, the effects of which I felt for some years. But is it possible my dear Brother can think my concern for him is merely for my own support? Can he not see that I am sensible he has already done for me beyond all reasonable expectation from me?"

Or perhaps he was angry with her for not showing his letter about Peter Collas to her daughter. "I therefore when she was affected at seeing me shed tears on reading your letter, determined to show it to her; and she says she is sincerely glad he did not git any goods there, as it must have increased his difficulties, and that she had not any suspicion of his making such an attempt. . . .

"Though I, neither, fear death as a misfortune to me, I wish to live long enough to receive from you a conviction, by your returning to your former style of writing to me, that you have forgiven my offense, whatsoever it is, for it would be terrible to me to imagine I had lost my dear Brother's affection while I remain in this life."

John Lathrop, minister of her church, brought her a letter written to him by Franklin. "I am glad," Franklin there said, "my dear sister has so good and kind a neighbor" as Lathrop. "I sometimes suspect she may be backward in acquainting me with circumstances in which I might be more useful to her. If any such should occur to your observation, your mentioning them to me will be a favor I shall be thankful for." Jane in a postscript to her letter said she had read the letter to Lathrop and was grateful for the "affectionate concern" her brother there expressed for her.

Then, after a week, she added another postscript before she sent her letter off. "I wrote the above the day after I received yours, but on reading it several times since I begin to doubt whether you were angry or no. If you were not, pray don't let this make you so, but impute all to a weakness of mind, depraved by *my* old age, which was never very strong."

II

During these years Jane Mecom came to depend upon John Lathrop for help and counsel in her affairs. Minister of the Second Church (the church of Increase and Cotton Mather) before the Revolution, Lathrop had come back from his exile to find the meeting house torn down by the British for firewood. The congregation merged with the congregation of the New Brick Church, in Hanover Street near Wood Lane (now Richmond Street); both bodies thereafter using the New Brick building and the Second (Old North) name. Jane Mecom, returning to Unity Street from her long exile, lived close to Christ Church, but that was Episcopalian. The Brattle Street Church, which she had formerly attended, was too far away. She became a member of Lathrop's church,

partly because of her liking for him. He was more than her
spiritual adviser. She had outlived not only her husband and
her sons and all her brothers except Benjamin, but also most
of her nephews; and Jonathan Williams, Sr., a nephew who
was almost her son, was now in bad health, failing in his business, and troubled in his mind. Lathrop, thirty years her
junior, became almost nephew as well as pastor to her; and
as he lived in North Square, he was a useful neighbor. She
had no hesitation about depending on him after she read her
brother's letter to Lathrop, asking him to watch over her.

She had need of him in the summer of 1788. "I have suffered a sore trial since I wrote to you," she told Franklin early
in September, "in the sickness of my granddaughter Jenny,
who is my constant attendant and comfort. For six weeks
my exercise of body and mind was so severe I had scare time
to think of anything else. For eight-and-forty hours we despaired of her life. Her physician said afterwards, though he
had long practice he had never a patient with all the symp-
toms of death on them as she had, that recovered. But thank
God she is again about house and we have hopes of perfect
recovery. I myself held out bravely, and we had the assistance
of a number of kind friends, and Providence so ordered it
that there was nothing necessary for her relief and comfort
but what it was in our power to procure and administer immediately."

During those same weeks Franklin was absorbed in writing the third part of his Memoirs (later known as his *Autobiography*) and wrote his sister no known letters till the
middle of September, when he remembered to send money
for her winter's wood. Thanking him later in the month, she
was happy to hear that after "a severe ill turn" he was now
in better health, and that Sarah Bache had another child.

"I rejoice with you and the other happy parents," Jane wrote, "in the increase of your family. It is said Mr. Bache is remarkable for having the finest children in Philadelphia. How much pleasure they must give you when you have ease to enjoy it! I long to have every one to kiss and play with that I see pass the street, that look clean and healthy. You did not give me the name. I think this is the seventh. Mrs. Bache may make up my number twelve, though she did not begin so young." Sarah Bache, given the name of her dead sister, was her mother's eighth and last child.

In the *Massachusetts Centinel* for November 1, Jane Mecom came upon an "Anecdote," ascribed to Franklin, which she remembered having read as he wrote it or, perhaps, having heard as he told it. It went back more than twenty years, to the days when Franklin was ridiculing the English argument that the Americans ought to pay for the stamps they ought to have used while the Stamp Act was in force and before it was repealed. "The whole proceeding," Franklin wrote, "would put one in mind of the Frenchman that used to accost English and other strangers on the Pont-Neuf, with many compliments and a red hot iron in his hand. 'Pray, Monsieur Anglois,' says he, 'do me the favor to let me have the honor of thrusting this hot iron into your backside.' 'Zoons, what does the fellow mean? Begone with your iron or I'll break your head.' 'Nay, Monsieur,' replies he, 'if you do not choose it, I do not insist upon it. But at least you will in justice have the goodness to pay me something for the heating of my iron.' "

The Boston version in the *Centinel* was loutishly told, with the mild profanity "d——n" three times in it. Jane Mecom, who did not object to the tavern quality of the anecdote, objected to the profanity now added. "I suppose you see our newspapers," she wrote her brother, "where you see how fond our people are to say something of Dr. Franklin, I believe mostly to do him honor. But some choose to embellish the language to their own fancy. The story of the Frenchman with the poker was a good story when you told it, but it appears to me there was none of your 'D——n your souls' in it."

Franklin pleasantly replied: "As you observe, there was no swearing in the story of the poker when I told it. The late new dresser of it was probably the same, or perhaps akin to him, who in relating a dispute that happened between Queen Anne and the Archbishop of Canterbury, concerning a vacant mitre which the Queen was for bestowing on a person the Archbishop thought unworthy, made both the Queen and the Archbishop swear three or four thumping oaths in every sentence of the discussion, and the Archbishop at last gained his point. One present at this tale, being surprised, said: 'But did the Queen and the Archbishop swear so at one another?' 'O no, no,' says the relator; 'that is only *my way* of telling the story.' "

The winter of 1788–89 was hard on both brother and sister, and from March or April he was most of the time confined to his bed by his malady. "During the extremely painful paroxysms," as his physician John Jones later recorded, Franklin "was obliged to take large doses of laudanum to mitigate his torture. Still, in the intervals of pain he not only amused himself with reading and conversing cheerfully with his family, and a few friends who visited him, but was often employed in doing business of a public as well as a private nature, with various persons who waited on him for that purpose; and in every instance displayed not only that readiness and disposition of doing good which was the distinguishing characteristic of his life, but the fullest and clearest possession of his uncommon mental abilities; and not unfrequently in-

dulged himself in those *jeux d'esprits* and entertaining anec-
dotes which were the delight of all who heard him."

To his sister, who had to guess or fear how bad he was, or
find out from others who tried to spare her, Franklin was
invariably serene in his few letters. "I am sorry you should
suffer so much uneasiness with tears and apprehensions about
my health," he wrote at the end of November 1788. "There are
in life real evils enough, and it is a folly to afflict ourselves
with imaginary ones; and it is time enough when the real
ones arrive. I see by the papers that tomorrow is your thanks-
giving day. The flour"—which he had sent her—"will arrive
too late for your plum puddings." In July 1789, in an interval
of pain, he wrote in resignation. "As to the pain I suffer, about
which you make yourself so unhappy, it is, when compared
with the long life I have enjoyed of health and ease, but a
trifle. And it is right that we should meet with something
to wean us from this world and make us willing, when called,
to leave it; otherwise the parting would indeed be grievous."

A series of mishaps led to a misunderstanding which came
as near to making Franklin sound vexed, though not with his
sister, as anything in their long correspondence. Benjamin
Franklin Bache, taught printing in Paris and now a printer
under his grandfather's direction in Philadelphia, published
in 1788 four small books by the English Anna Letitia Barbauld. *Mrs. Barbauld's Lessons for Children*, of different ages,
with alterations, the title page read, *suited to the American
Climate*. Franklin sent a shipment of the books for sale in
Boston, consigning them to Jonathan Williams, Sr. Williams
for some reason sent them to Jane Mecom, who was to share
in the profits of the sale. She had difficulty in disposing of
them, as she reported in a missing letter to her brother. "It
was not my intention," he said in February, "you should have

any trouble with them: as you will see by the enclosed copy of my letter to Cousin Williams. By his sending them to you, it seems as if there was some misunderstanding between you, or that he is tired of rendering you services. If you do not find some bookseller who will buy them of you in a lump, I think you had better pack them up and send them back again." Williams had failed to answer Franklin's letter, "which confirms my impression of there being some miff. . . . As to the books themselves, how much soever your people may despise them, they are really valuable for the purpose of teaching children to read. The largeness and plainness of the character [type] and the little sentences of common occurrences which they can understand when they read, make them delight in reading them so as to forward their progress exceedingly. Our little Richard, not yet five years old, has by their means outstript his brother Lewis in reading, who is near nine."

This letter, and others on the same subject addressed "To Mrs. Mecom, Unity Street, Boston," did not reach her till late in July, after Franklin had written her yet another letter, in care of Williams. Then, Jane replied, "Cousin Williams came immediately down to me with the letter, as he always does, and finding you had sent so many that I had not received, he went in the morning to the [post] office and they made a shift to find two, but that dated May is not to be found. They say they did not know there was such a person" as Jane Mecom "in town, and that they had advertised them. But this is not the first time they have served me so by several. They are too lazy to look. For my granddaughter has asked at the office many times in this space of time. I have formerly been told there were letters there for me, and when I sent there was none; sent a second time by some one who would stand by and force them to look, and got them. . . .

"Their misconduct has led you to a great mistake concerning Cousin Williams. There never was a person more assiduous in their endeavors to oblige than he has always been to me. We never had a word with each other that had the least appearance of miff in it; and he says he can lay his hand on his heart and say it has always been the greatest pleasure to him to have it in his power to render me any service, and it has always appeared so to me. . . . Mr. Williams says he was to blame in not writing at the time" the books arrived; "but that he was very unwell and his mind so discomposed with trouble he could not have set about writing to you. He is really grieved that you should have such a suspicion of him."

Roused by so many letters from Franklin, and with this opportunity to forget his illness, Jane went on in the gossiping vein that had not lately appeared in her letters.

"Sukey Hubbart was buried the night before last; and we have a neighbor now lies dead, the last of the old set of inhabitants of this street: Mrs. Larrabee. There has been one or two deaths in every house in the street since we came to live here, ours only exempt. We have no reason to expect it will remain so long."

The story of Peter Collas had now another chapter. Finally shipping as mate on a vessel to the West Indies and South Carolina, "he was not able to leave his wife more than twenty dollars when he went away, which was but small to supply the family and his wife with what necessaries she wanted for her own person. All but that has lain wholly on me ever since, till about a fortnight ago he sent her a small supply from Carolina. This being the case, I was careful to live frugally and have not been very much straitened till the very instant her money came. But I had unavoidably contracted a large debt for my granddaughter's sickness a year ago which I have not been able to pay. . . . On this account, and to indulge myself in a few little things, I will thankfully accept the forty dollars" her brother had sent, "as I see no probable prospect of paying this debt without it; and a debt is a burden I cannot bear. I owe no one else a farthing except a little back rates for my pew at meeting, which I have not been asked for."

She ended with a postscript: "If my dear Brother would add to his superscriptions of his letters 'At the back of the North Church,' I might git them the readier." (By "North Church" she here meant Christ Church, years later the "Old North Church" of Paul Revere's ride in the poem.) After that Franklin sent his letters in care of Jonathan Williams.

Franklin, well enough to reply at once, thought the Boston post office "very badly managed." Jonathan Williams, Jr., was now in Boston. "I would have you," Franklin said, "put the books into Cousin Jonathan's hands, who will dispose of them for you if he can, or return them hither. I am very much pleased to hear that you have had no misunderstanding with his good father. Indeed, if there had been any such, I should have concluded it was your fault; for I think our family were always subject to being a little miffy. By the way, is our relalationship in Nantucket quite worn out? I have met with none from thence of late years who were disposed to be acquainted with me, except Captain Timothy Folger. They are wonderfully shy. But I admire their honest plainness of speech. About a year ago I invited two of them to dine with me. Their answer was that they would—*if* they could do no better. I suppose they did better, for I never saw them afterward, and so had no opportunity of showing my miff, if I had one. Give my love to Cousin Williams's and thank them for me for all the kindnesses to you, which I have always been acquainted with by you, and take as if done to myself. . . . I shall make the addition you desire to my superscriptions, desiring in return that you make a subtraction from yours. The word 'Excellency' does not belong to me," now that he was no longer President of Pennsylvania, "and 'Dr.' will be sufficient to distinguish me from my grandson."

He said nothing about money, but he had that year in a codicil to his will increased his annuity to her, after his death, from fifty to sixty pounds.

Now for the rest of 1789 letters went back and forth more regularly between them. "You introduce your reproof of my miffy temper," she wrote in August, "so politely one can't avoid wishing to have conquered it as you have, if you ever had any, that disagreeable temper." She had not put the "Excellency" in her address, but had left her letters to be addressed by Dr. Lathrop, "who is very obliging to me. . . . He desires always to be respectfully remembered to you when I write.

"I believe there are a few of our Nantucket relations who have still an affection for us, but the war time, which made such havoc everywhere, divided and scattered them about. Those I was most intimate with were Abisha Folger, his brothers and sons (Timothy one), the Jenkinses, and Kezia Coffin, who was many years like a sister to me and a great friend to my children. She sent me two very affectionate letters when the town was shut up, inviting me to come to her and she would sustain me—that was her word; and had I received them before I left the town I should certainly have gone. But a wise and good Providence ordered it otherways. She took to the wrong side and exerted herself by every method

she could devise, right or wrong, to accomplish her designs
and favor the British; went into large trade with them, and
for them, and by mismanagement and not succeeding in her
endeavors has sunk every farthing they were ever possessed
of, and have been in jail both, her husband at Nantucket and
herself at Halifax. She was always thought to be an artful
woman, but there are such extraordinary stories told of her as
is hard to be believed."

Jane told how Kezia Coffin had directed a loyalist raiding
party (from New York) to the warehouse of Seth and Thomas
Jenkins, and "robbed them of all. . . . The owners prose-
cuted her, and she was brought up to Boston to stand trial;
but I think there was no final condemnation at court. She
says they could not find evidence. They say the evidence was
so strong that had they suffered them to come into court it
would have hanged her; and so they suppressed it, not being
willing it should proceed so far." They were all related through
the Folger strain. The Jenkinses, settled in Rhode Island for
a time, had entertained Jane Mecom at their house in Providence: "sent their sons to carry me from there to my grandson's thirteen miles in their chaise, and every other obliging
thing in their power. . . . I have not seen a Nantucket person since I lived here" in Unity Street.

Late in November she heard from their cousin John Williams, just returned from Philadelphia, that her brother was
"as cheerful and as merry and seem[s] as well as ever at times,
and that you say your pains in common are not so exquisite
as formerly." Herself cheered by this, she sent him *A Sermon
on Sacred Music* by Ezra Weld, which she thought "a pretty
discourse from a country minister who has every circumstance
to depress him." With the sermon she sent a question some
friend had asked her to submit to Franklin: "whether the

general circumstances mentioned in the history of Baron Trenck are founded on fact."

Franklin's reply came back prompt and clear, beginning with a request which he knew would delight her. "I have lately wished to regale on cod's tongues and sounds [the fish's swimming bladders]; and if you could now and then send me a small keg of them, containing about two quarts, they would be very acceptable to your affectionate brother." He had liked these delicacies as a boy in Boston, and his sister, sending them, would remember their childhood.

Baron Trenck was a Prussian soldier of fortune whose swaggering *Life* was just then being read in numerous editions in German, French, and English in both Europe and America. One of his tall tales said, in the English version: "From the year 1774 to 1777 I chiefly spent my time in journeying through England and France. I was intimate with Dr. Franklin, the American minister; also with the Counts St. Germain and Vergennes, who made me advantageous proposals to go to America; but I was prevented accepting them by my affection for my wife and children." On this Franklin must be the chief authority in the United States.

"You tell me," he wrote his sister, "you are desired by an acquaintance to ask my opinion whether the general circumstances in the history of Baron Trenck are founded in fact; to which I can only answer, that of the greatest part of those circumstances, the scene being laid in Germany, I must consequently be very ignorant; but of what he says as having passed in France, between the ministers of that country, himself, and me, I can speak positively that it is *founded* on falsehood, and that the fact can only serve to *con*found it, as I never saw him in that country, nor ever knew or heard of him anywhere till I met with the mentioned history in print, in the

German language, in which he ventured to relate it as a fact that I had with those ministers solicited him to enter into the American service. A translation of that book into French has since been printed, but the translator has omitted that pretended fact, probably from an apprehension that its being, in that country, known not to be true might hurt the credit and sale of the translation."

Franklin had read the *Sermon on Sacred Music,* and thanked his sister for it. "I have read it with pleasure—I think it a very ingenious composition. You will say this is natural enough, if you read what I have formerly written on the same subject in one of my printed letters, wherein you will find a perfect agreement of sentiment respecting the complex music of late, in my opinion, too much in vogue, it being only pleasing to learned ears who can be delighted with the difficulty of execution instead of simple harmony and melody." If Jane looked up what he had written, in the collection of his writings sent her twenty years before, she noted again that his opinion of complex music was in the form of a letter to their brother Peter, who had once composed a ballad.

III

Franklin in his final year was quietly saying farewell to his closest friends. In March 1789 he concluded his last letter to Catharine Greene with: "Among the felicities of my life I reckon your friendship, which I shall remember with pleasure as long as that life lasts." She spoke of the letter to Jane Mecom, who told her brother in July: "Our friend Mrs. Greene received your letter. She calls it a dear good letter and says she will bring it when she comes to see me in the fall." Then in November: "Our good old friend Mrs. Greene has been to see me. To our great mortification she has somehow mislaid your letter. She thought she brought it, but finds herself mistaken."

On Franklin's birthday in 1790, sixty-three years to the day after his earliest letter to his sister, Jane wrote him: "This day my dear Brother completes his eighty-fourth year. You cannot, as old Jacob, say few and evil have they been, except those wherein you have endured such grievous torments latterly. Yours have been filled with innumerable good works, benefits to your fellow creatures, and thankfulness to God; [so] that notwithstanding the distressing circumstances before mentioned, yours must be esteemed a glorious life. Great increase of glory and happiness I hope await you. May God mitigate your pain and continue your patience yet many years. For who that know and love you can bear the thought of surviving you in this gloomy world?

"I esteem it very fortunate that Cousin John Williams is returning to Philadelphia again and will take a keg of sounds and tongues by land, as there is no vessel likely to go till March. I have tasted them and think them very good. Shall as long as they are acceptable send you fresh and fresh as I have opportunity.

"I am as you suppose six years younger than you are, being born on the 27th March 1712, but to appearance in every one's sight as much older." This is the only reference to her looks she ever made in a known letter. Nor did her brother ever make any besides his teasing comment, when she was forty-seven: "You fatfolks can't bear malice."

"We have hitherto," she went on, "a very moderate winter, but I do not attempt to go abroad. My breath just serves me to go about the house without great pain. And as I am comfortable at home, I strive to be content."

On February 6, in reply to a missing letter from him in which he said she had sent a larger quantity of tongues and sounds than he had expected, she explained: "I was very sure there was danger of your being disgusted with the quantity I sent, but was overruled; but determined not to send more at a time for the future than you mentioned. I hope how [ever] you have been able to regale on them more than once, as I believe they are so thoroughly preserved they will remain sweet all the cool weather. I bless God for all the intervals of ease you have, and am your affectionate sister." This was her last letter to him.

In March he had an astounding interval of ease that permitted him on the ninth to write his famous letter on his religious beliefs to Ezra Stiles, and on the twenty-third his spirited parody *On the Slave Trade* in which "the dying philosopher feathered his last arrow with a wit still light and swift." On the twenty-fourth he wrote his last letter to Jane Mecom.

"I received your kind letter by your good neighbor, Captain [Obadiah] Rich," who lived in Unity Street. "The information it contained, that you continue well, gave me, as usual, great pleasure. As to myself, I have been quite free from pain for near three weeks past; and therefore not being obliged to take any laudanum, my appetite has returned, and I have recovered some part of my strength. Thus I continue to live on, while all the friends of my youth have left me, and gone to join the majority. I have, however, the pleasure of continued friendship and conversation with their children and grandchildren. I do not repine at my malady, though a severe one, when I consider how well I am provided with every convenience to palliate it and to make me comfortable under it; and how many more horrible evils the human body is subject to; and what a long life of health I have been blessed with, free from them all.

"You have done well not to send me any more fish at present. These continue good, and give me pleasure.

"Do you know anything of our Sister Scott's daughter; whether she is still living, and where? This family join in love to you and yours, and to Cousin Williams, with your affectionate brother, B. Franklin."

"P. S. It is early in the morning, and I write in bed. The awkward position has occasioned the crooked lines."

After that Franklin wrote only one surviving letter: to Thomas Jefferson, Secretary of State in Washington's cabinet, about the map which had been used in making the treaty of peace with England. Before the earliest letter from Franklin to Jane Mecom, on his twenty-first birthday, he had written only one other that has survived: to Sir Hans Sloane, benefactor of the British Museum, about some curiosities of natural history the youth had brought to London from North America. His correspondence opened with science and closed with diplomacy, but between those first and last letters he wrote more letters to his sister, and over a longer period of years, than to any other person.

These facts the grieving woman in Unity Street could not know; nor is she likely ever to have wondered whether any other woman—mother, sister, wife, daughter, lover, or dear friend—had meant as much to Franklin as she herself had.

11

To Its Parent Dust

NOBODY now knows how the shattering news of Franklin's death on April 17 came to Jane Mecom. Unless the general report outran the message sent by Richard Bache on the nineteenth, she first heard of it when some friend of his and hers called on her in Unity Street, with a few words gently spoken, and then Bache's letter.

"My duty calls upon me," she read, "to make you acquainted with an event which I know will be a sore affliction to your affectionate breast. And lest the news should reach you and be communicated to you in an abrupt manner, and that your tender feelings might still be more wounded, I have thought it best to enclose these few lines to a friend who I hope will first prepare you for the shock. Amidst the affliction of a distressed family I am hardly connected enough to offer any consolation. My condolence at present must suffice; and, my dear Madam, I do most sincerely condole with you on the loss of so excellent a friend and brother. I have not time at present to add more than that he died on Saturday last at ten o'clock at night. He had not been long very ill, and therefore we had hardly an opportunity of informing you of it; besides, we had been in daily expectation of his getting better. But nature was at last worn out. I beg of you to look upon me as your

sincere friend, and as one who will be very happy in rendering you any services in his power."

If she cried out, her voice is long silent; if she wept, her
tears are long dry. Only a few weeks before she had written
her brother: "Who that know and love you can bear the
thoughts of surviving you in this gloomy world?" Today she
had more than thoughts to bear.

She took what comfort she could from the consoling friends
who visited her, and from the praise of her brother that
quickly filled the newspapers. He was in 1790 the greatest
American who had ever died, the greatest man who had ever
died in the United States. "The concourse of spectators" at
his funeral, the *Massachusetts Centinel* said on May 1, "was
greater than ever was known on the like occasion." For weeks
his fame was the news in Boston, in prose and verse. There
was his will, in which he left a hundred pounds sterling to
the "free schools in my native town," the interest to be an-
nually "laid out in silver medals" for pupils who deserved
them; and a thousand pounds sterling to "the inhabitants
of the town of Boston" as a fund to be lent at interest to young
tradesmen and the interest compounded for two hundred
years: "not presuming to carry my views farther." On May
26 the *Centinel* printed the anecdote of Franklin in his boyhood, when, tired of long graces before meat, he proposed
that grace be said over the whole meat tub at once, to save
time. Who in Boston remembered that better than Jane Mecom? In August came the eulogy of Franklin that Mirabeau
had pronounced before the National Assembly of France.
"Antiquity would have raised altars," Mirabeau said, "to this
mighty genius, who, to the advantage of mankind, compass-
ing in his mind the heavens and the earth, was able to restrain
alike thunderbolts and tyrants."

Out of the crowd of voices Jane Mecom is first heard in a
letter she wrote on September 6 to Sarah Bache. "It is a cordial
to my heart to receive such affectionate notice from my dear
brother's child. He while living was to me every enjoyment.
Whatever other pleasures were, as they mostly took their rise
from him, they passed like little streams from a beautiful
fountain. They remind me of two lines of a song Mr. Peters
used to sing at your house:

But now they are withered and waned all away.

"To make society agreeable there must be a similarity of
circumstances and sentiments, as well as age. I have no such
near me; my dear brother supplied all. Every line from him
was a pleasure. If I asked questions he did not think proper
to inform me on, he would sometimes give me a gentle reproof.
At other times he entirely passed it over; that I knew was always fitted for the occasion, and all was pleasure.

But now they are withered and waned all away.

"It is, however, very agreeable to me to see there is hardly
a newspaper comes out in this town without honorable mention of him; and indeed it is a fund that cannot be exhausted."
She hoped that Benjamin Franklin Bache, just then estab-
lishing his newspaper the *General Advertiser,* would succeed
in his undertaking; "but it seems to me a vast one. May he
inherit all his grandfather's virtues, and then he will be likely
to succeed to his honors. I hope he will remember his old aunt
with a present of some of his papers, when convenient. . . .
"When I sit down to write to you I think I will try to correct
my writing and spelling; but I am grown so infirm and so
indolent the task is too arduous. If you can find out what I

mean, you must accept it as it is; if not, let me know, and I will get my daughter to write for me."

She wrote again on December 2. "I hear my dear brother's will is printed. I wish you would send me one of them." She had seen a copy of her nephew's newspaper. "It appears to me very respectable. If his Wednesday's paper fills equally it may soon create for him an estate in the clouds, as his venerable grandfather used to say of his newspaper debts."

After that no letters from Jane Mecom survive except three, in her daughter's handwriting but signed by the mother, to the executors of Franklin's will and about the legacies to his sister. In one of the letters in August 1791 she spoke of the fifty pounds sterling "to be divided between the whole number" of her descendants, "which were sixteen living at my brother's death. If it could be done without difficulty or impropriety, I should desire only such a part as belongs to my daughter Jane Collas, my granddaughter Jane Mecom, my grandson Josiah Flagg of Lancaster, and two great-grandchildren Sarah and Franklin Greene living at Rhode Island, from whom we have a power"—of attorney—"to be sent this way. My daughter and myself will give a full discharge for that sum and engage to deliver it. All the others are there at Philadelphia except one at Amboy, Mrs. Elizabeth Mecom's daughter Abiah Mecom."

The ten at Philadelphia were the son and three other daughters of Elizabeth Mecom, and their children: making, with Jane in Boston and Abiah in Amboy, a dozen descendants of the distracted Benjamin Mecom who had been lost in the freezing December of 1776 and never heard of again.

The death of Franklin broke the mirror in which much of Jane Mecom's life had been recorded, but certain later traces of it appear in the records of the property he gave or be-

queathed her. With her house and sixty pounds a year she
lived in the decent comfort she liked. A year after his death
she had £290 at interest in personal loans, one for £70 to her
grandson Elihu Greene. Her son-in-law Collas seems to have
left the scene. Jane Collas continued to be languishing, Jenny
Mecom amiable and hearty. The eldest of the Jane Mecoms,
when she was not too much racked by her asthmatic cough,
was free to work or rest or read or converse as she pleased,
in a pleasant house which was her own.

In her parlor, which was also her dining room on ceremonial
occasions, she had two stuffed-back easy chairs and a scal-
loped mahogany tea table, as well as the square mahogany
dining table and eight leather-bottom chairs that went with
it. The andirons, shovel, and tongs at the fireplace were brass;
the dozen teaspoons, punch ladle, and two tablespoons silver;
the butter boats and candlesticks plated. There were china,
glass, and delftware on the buffet, and a Scotch carpet on the
floor.

In her chamber above the parlor, with two windows facing
the morning sun, she had her own bed with its tester and curtains and another for her granddaughter who shared the room.
There were a chest of drawers and a table; a toilet table and
brushes; a fine looking glass; a cane-back armchair and other
chairs not specified; a child's desk (what child's, and from
how long ago?); a mahogany beausoir; a mahogany close stool
and frame; two pieces of carpeting on the floor; four pictures,
and perhaps a fifth, most of them probably of Franklin; and,
according to the inventory after her death, "5 Volumes of
Books."

Jane Collas's room at the rear was less handsomely furnished, though on this point the inventory is not so clear. In

the kitchen there was a tea table for ordinary family meals, and ample equipment for the fire and cooking. The cellar smelled of cider and small beer and pork laid down for the winter.

Not a word from her in these last years about who called on her or whom she visited; who wrote her letters or whom she replied to; how cold the winter was or how hot the summer; what she read or wished to read. Her favorite niece, Grace Williams, died just before Franklin. Jane Mecom felt desolate when the Baches in 1792 left Philadelphia to see Richard Bache's family in England and Franklin's friends wherever the two traveled. "I have no brother, son, nor nephew near me," to help her in her affairs, she wrote to one of Franklin's executors in July 1793. She sent the executor a keg of pickled lobsters. "I am told they are very nice; hope they will prove so and beg your acceptance . . . of them."

In January 1794 Catharine Greene, Jane Mecom's closest friend and young enough to be her daughter, died at Warwick. There was a notice of the death in the *Boston Gazette* for February 17. And on that day Jane Mecom made her will.

"I, Jane Mecom of Boston in the County of Suffolk and Commonwealth of Massachusetts, Widow; being, although weak in body, yet of sound mind and memory; well knowing that the time must arise when I shall be called upon to resign this decaying frame to its parent dust, and my spirit to the GOD who gave it; do this seventeenth day of February in the year of Our Lord One thousand seven hundred and ninety four, ordain, make and publish this my Last will and testament, in manner following."

Most of the preamble was in the legal form then customary, but the words "the time must arise when I shall be called upon to resign this decaying frame to its parent dust" have the ring of the testator's own style and seem as clearly hers as the firm signature at the end.

Her first bequest, to Josiah Flagg now forgiven for his offenses, was "my silver porringer marked P F M," once her mad son Peter's, and ten pounds in money. The second was to the great-grandchildren Franklin Greene ("my gold sleeve buttons") and Sarah Greene ("a mourning ring which was given me at the funeral of my kinsman Josiah Williams"— that grandnephew who had been so promising a musician but who had come home from England to die in his twenties).

Then there was a bequest whose details almost open the door of the home in Unity Street and half reveal the household. "In consideration of the extraordinary attention paid me by my Grand daughter Jane Mecom, exclusive of her common and necessary concerns in domestic affairs and the ordinary business of the family, I think proper to give and bequeath unto her several articles of household furniture, particularly, as follows.—The Bed, Bedstead and Curtains which I commonly use; the three pair of homespun sheets lately made, and the bedding of every kind used with this bed both in Summer and winter; consisting of two blankets, a white Counter pane and two Calico bed quilts, one of which is new;—The Chest of Drawers and table which usually stand in my Chamber, and six black walnut chairs with green bottoms; also two black chairs; my looking glass which I bought of Samuel Taylor, and which commonly hangs in my Chamber; a large brass kettle, a small bell mettle skillet [which had been in the Hanover Street boarding house when Edward Mecom died], a small iron pot, a large trammel, a pair of large iron hand-irons, a shovel and pair of Tongs, a black walnut stand and Tea-board, two brass candlesticks, a small copper tea kettle and one half of my wearing apparel of every kind, which I desire may be divided by Mrs Elizabeth Lathrop and Miss Abigail Woodman and any other friend whom they may chuse to assist them in the business— and also the sum of Ten Pounds L M"—that is, lawful money of Massachusetts, the money plainly added as an afterthought.

Here was enough to furnish two rooms decently for the devoted granddaughter who had given her youth to Jane Mecom, with things which would remind her of her grandmother and her gratitude.

The house and lot were left to John Lathrop, D.D., and Benjamin Sumner, merchant, to be held in trust for the use of Jane Collas, who might live there, or have any rent or income produced "during the term of her natural life." If the rent or income should not be sufficient to support and maintain her comfortably, then the trustees might give her outright any part of the personal property not bequeathed to other heirs, or pledge the real estate for such an amount "as may in their opinions be necessary to her comfortable maintenance and support." In other words, here only implied, the property, personal or real, was not to be entrusted to the limp hands of Jane Collas or the slippery hands of her husband, if he was still alive.

After the death of Jane Collas, all the remaining property, real and personal, was to be sold and divided in two parts: one part to be divided equally among Josiah Flagg and Sarah and Franklin Greene, the other part among the children, here not named, "of my son Benjamin Mecom deceased."

To Mrs. Elizabeth Lathrop, John Lathrop's second wife, was bequeathed for her trouble in dividing the wearing apparel "a white medallion of Dr. Franklin"—presumably the

Wedgwood "head" he had sent his sister from England. For Abigail Woodman, a member of Jane Mecom's church and keeper of a toy shop in the neighborhood, there was for some reason no bequest. The witnesses to the will were two neighbor women, Martha Rob and Achsah Lombard, and John Lathrop, Jr., son of the minister by his first wife, a young lawyer and poet. There was not a Franklin "cousin" among them. Jane Mecom had not only outlived all her brothers and sisters but had also outlived, or outgrown, all their children.

On March 3 the *Boston Gazette* printed an extract from a letter of Franklin "to a friend in Boston, not long before his death." The extract was on the folly of war, and the letter the one her brother had written to Jane Mecom at the close of the Federal Convention. If she was giving up his letters to public eyes, she knew she was near the end of her life. It was probably in these days that she presented about twenty-five of his letters to an otherwise unidentified Mrs. Hawk (or Hawkes), from whom they passed into a strange obscurity not finally ended till 1950.

In Jane Mecom's last sickness she was attended by Dr. Isaac Rand, a Boston physician who had openly opposed the Revolution without ever losing the confidence and respect of his many patients who admired him for his skill and kindness. How death actually came to her is not known or even on what day. The *Columbian* (formerly *Massachusetts*) *Centinel* for May 10 had a death and funeral notice in which her name, so far as has been known, first appeared in print. "Mrs. Jane Mecom, widow of the late Mr. Edward Mecom of this town, and the only sister of the late Doctor Franklin, in the 83d year of her age. Her funeral will be this afternoon, precisely at five o'clock, from her late dwelling near the North Church, which her friends, and the friends of the late Dr.

Franklin, are requested to attend." What friends attended, or whether John Lathrop conducted the services, or where she was buried are not known.

Her estate, valued at about a thousand pounds, was enough to maintain her daughter Jane Collas in reasonable comfort for the eight years she lived, apparently in the care of her niece Jenny Mecom, and yet leave about half of it to be divided among the grandchildren and great-grandchildren in the final settlement. Jenny, the youngest Jane Mecom, two years before Jane Collas's death married Captain Simeon Kinsman. She outlived him and all the Mecom grandchildren, and was still alive in 1859.

The house in Unity Street, sold in 1802, survived with various alterations till 1939, when it was torn down to enlarge the vista along the Paul Revere Mall between Christ Church and St. Stephen's in Hanover Street. The site of the house and the one adjoining it on the south have been enclosed in a small garden with a wall and a gate. In the Mall, with its fountain and the statue of Paul Revere on his horse, a bronze plaque informs the sightseer that the house formerly standing at 19 Unity Street at the head of the Mall was owned by Benjamin Franklin and "occupied by his sisters," without a name for Elizabeth Douse or Jane Mecom.

But the name of Jane Mecom survives in the love and the letters between her and her brother. To her he was the overshadowing hero of their story, but she was a heroine herself. Of all the Franklins the youngest daughter was the only one who had some of the immortal quality of the youngest son. Benjamin was a man. With his young, strong talents he could make and charm his way in the world and early rise above the hampering circumstances of his youth. Jane was a woman, hard beset by early marriage, early and long poverty, many children, many hardships, many bereavements as her sons died young or grew languid or went mad, and her most promising daughters died almost before they could begin to live. If it is a wonder that Jane Mecom lived at all, it is a miracle that she lived through her dark vicissitudes, as Franklin lived through his enormous labors, and that she came at last to an old age of triumph: after a day so long and stormy, an evening relatively serene and pleasant.

As in her long life she never tired of him, so he never tired of her. Something in her valiant, upright spirit, with so much woman and so much mind in it, made her his peculiar favorite from her babyhood. On his busiest days, in Philadelphia, London, Paris, he thought of her, and was comforted by the security the thought gave him. He took pains to win and keep her good opinion of his public conduct. Though he said little to her of his scientific achievements, which she understood hardly at all, this was to spare her any least embarrassment. With her he could turn aside whenever he liked from his complicated duties and talk cheerfully with her of shared old memories or present difficulties and satisfactions or domestic hopes for the future. Their love and their letters, reaching back and forth between them, bound them together in the longest comfortable friendship either of them ever had.

Without the letters, the love might have been lost sight of. It shines in all his words, whether he advised or consoled or teased her. Within her range, and in her own bright, ardent, impetuous, sometimes faulty idiom, she wrote almost as well as he, with a touch of flavor and distinction in every line. Their correspondence is the conversation of a wise man and a sensitive, emotional woman, about the things that mattered to them jointly, through all the changes of their differing fortunes, for more than sixty years. That correspondence, much of it long buried, now comes to light in words as true and colors as lively as they ever were. Jane Mecom adds a new grace to Benjamin Franklin. He mirrors and interprets her. Hereafter neither brother nor sister will stand alone in the world's memory, for neither can be fully known or truly remembered without the other.

Acknowledgment

With the kind permission of The American Philosophical Society this biography of Jane Mecom draws freely upon letters and documents published by or for the Society in *Benjamin Franklin and Catharine Ray Greene: Their Correspondence 1755–1790* (Philadelphia: American Philosophical Society, 1949), edited by William Greene Roelker, and *The Letters of Benjamin Franklin and Jane Mecom* (Princeton University Press, 1950), edited by Carl Van Doren. Permission to make further use in the biography of materials which The American Philosophical Society was permitted to include in those correspondences is due, and is gratefully acknowledged, to The Library of Harvard University, The New England Historic Genealogical Society, The Massachusetts Historical Society, The Yale University Library, The New York Public Library, The Princeton University Library, The Library Company of Philadelphia, The Historical Society of Pennsylvania, and the Henry E. Huntington Library and Art Gallery, San Marino, California. Certain topographical details of modern Boston have been generously supplied by Dale Warren and Craig Wylie. Without the researches of Mary Barnard this book could not have been written. Without the affectionate advice of Mark Van Doren, who read the manuscript chapter by chapter as it came, the narrative would have lacked important narrative qualities which it owes to him.

Index